TIME-CRUNCHED
TRIATHLON

TIME-CRUNCHED TRIATHLON

JOE BEER

ROBERT HALE

First published in 2016 by
Robert Hale, an imprint of
The Crowood Press Ltd
Ramsbury, Marlborough
Wiltshire SN8 2HR

www.crowood.com

www.halebooks.com

British Library Cataloguing-in-Publication Data
A catalogue record for this book is available from the British Library.

ISBN 978 0 7198 1263 7

Typeset by Eurodesign

Printed and bound in India by Replika Press Pvt Ltd

For Seth, Ned & Iris

You give my life completeness

Contents

Foreword

Being a triathlete is not just simply training and racing – it can be a lifestyle choice for most, too. Managing the logistics of a cost-effective training plan specific to your own needs can be the difference from plateauing or taking the next step. Most regular triathletes need to have a good handle on what's realistic for them when all daily influences have been considered, then have a training plan that is specifically tailored for them to allow them to progress safely and with confidence.

Working a day job, studying, local weather, the climate, family commitments, social life – these all play a big part of our lives, so your time is valuable and should be invested wisely.

It's not who does the most, but who can optimize their training the best. You can achieve more for less by setting realistic monthly or yearly targets and by developing your training plan with rational thought.

When all added together, small margins can equal big progress. This can be done by honing sleep or bedtime routines, sticking to the plan by taking planned recovery days or even weeks, dialling in good nutrition and tweaking race equipment – they all play a big part of being the best triathlete you can be.

Time-Crunched Triathlon is not a 'one-read, put-down book' – rather it is something to go back to time and time again as a resource to enhance your triathlon experience.

Triathlon is a challenging sport; it's never easy – but *Time-Crunched Triathlon* certainly makes it easier.

SCOTT NEYEDLI, *winner of Ironman UK 2007 and Ironman Wales 2013*

9

Acknowledgements

I would like to thank Scott UK, PowerBar UK, InfoCrank, InDurance 220 Triathlon, Club La Santa Lanzarote, Speedo UK, Neovite, Yellowfield, Dry Robe, CEP Sports, Vasa and Lumie. I am very proud to be associated with each of you – your support is invaluable.

Without the help of Jonny Gawler (photography), Lavinia Porter (manuscript editing and dealing with me for months on end), Activity Wales (pictures) and the athletes in the photographs, this book would have been visually boring and full of bad English. So, thank you.

To the many athletes who have put their trust in me to help them become smarter, faster and more complete performers: you have taught me so much more than the textbooks, research papers or theories out there. Be your best.

To my friends, family, mentors and heroes. Every one of you has made amazing differences to the person I have become over the past three decades. I am forever in your debt.

To my mother and father: your hard work gave me the chances you never had. You're always supportive.

Picture Credits

The author and publisher wish to thank the following individuals for permission to reproduce their images (page numbers given in **bold**)

Scott Neyedli [**9**]
Gideon Bright [**20, 57**]
Activity Wales [**13, 161**]
Steve Walton [**110**]
Chris Goodfellow [**188**]

All remaining images taken by Jonny Gawler

CHAPTER ONE

Triathlon: It's Simpler than You Think

Once, people would step back in awe if someone announced that they were a triathlete. In those days, triathletes were super-beings whose fitness knew no bounds. They ate eat nails for breakfast and would train more than 24 hours a day – *never* with a rest day. While others were mere runners and rugby players, cyclists and surfers – triathletes were definitely members of the super-elite.

However, as time has passed, more and more people with everyday jobs have managed to complete a triathlon and the impossible super-sport is now open to all. Triathlon is very 'doable'. Triathlons are completed by that man sitting two desks away from you, or that woman at the end of the queue for the cash-till.

Each day people train and compete in triathlon. It's cool to be a Jack (or Jill) of three trades doing events like the Long Course Weekend in Wales.

Here's an amazing secret I found out by accident before I had ever read a gruelling story-book about triathlon, or seen a race portrayed as being impossible:

A triathlon is just a swim, followed by a bike ride,
followed by a run or walk to the finish.

And, as a kid, let's face it, we would have been doing some of these activities from time to time in any case, wouldn't we? We may not have been on a talent programme or bred as triathletes, but these are *not* 'impossible-to-enter' sports. So, as a teenager, I figured it was fine to enter triathlon. It's 'just three sports and a bit of changing-time' my young brain rationalized.

Fast-forward thirty years from that revelation, and those now entering triathlon (or continuing to compete as their life gets ever busier) are typically 30- and 40-somethings – not youngsters living off the 'Bank of Mum and Dad'. Nor are they 'fitness freaks' with nothing but triathlon on their minds. The triathlete of the twenty-first century is a busy man or woman living life to the full. As a result, they will often be squeezed for time – or *time-crunched*. If this sounds like you, help is at hand. With this book you can be an effective, happy and balanced multi-sporter – something, in hindsight, that many of the pioneers of the sport failed to do correctly. Learn from them – be triathlon-savvy.

Using the non-impact and practical qualities of biking can transform triathlon training into a time-saving commute or a way to complete errands – at speed!

Fundamentally, being triathlon-savvy is about being smart with your time, methods and equipment. Long training hours or jumping on each new piece of technology may give you gains in the short term. However, rational training progression, emphasis on recovery and adaptation, relevant equipment upgrades, and many other of the 'smart' habits mentioned in this book are the very best way forward. It has taken me many years, but I think I have the answers, so learn from my experience – it's all here for you.

Time-Crunched Triathlon has been designed to help you get to know and be able to store the essential information for later, without any need for electricity or a software upgrade. It will outline problem scenarios you'll come across and strategies for how you can resolve them – for example, how to train effectively in winter, how to cope with illness or work through training-staleness. This book simplifies cutting-edge research and sports science into powerful, easy-to-follow habits and systems. You don't need to know what exactly the ATP-CP system is; nor do you have to try to understand all the data on carbohydrate absorption across the gut. I've done it for you – happily – so you can focus on getting to be the very best you can be as a triathlete.

My central reason for doing endurance sport, for becoming a coach, and for writing about sport for over two decades is simple, but it's hard-wired into my DNA:

Many athletes come to triathlon for the variety, for the challenge, to stave off injury – or even for all three reasons.

> *I passionately want to blend powerful knowledge with directed toil to give the best results for you.*

Welcome to being your best! Being time-crunched is not going to stop us ....

Freeing Your Mind

Your brain is not the best place to keep things.

There's a lot going on in your head during the average day. Training planned this week, the bike route of your next race – and then there's that new session your friend just found on the internet. You can't keep every one of these in your head all day long. For a start, you have to think about what's going on in everyday life – like that mentally taxing project at work or how to keep up with the kids on the latest *Star Wars* Wii game. Your mind can't be just thinking 'triathlon' every minute of the day (see Chapter 11 right away if it is). Most importantly, your brain is never just a place to store the thousands of items that make up good multi-sport outcomes. Triathlon is made up of three sports; there are tons of ideas circulating the internet; and there's a new product every minute, every hour, every day. If you try to hold all that in your head, your training, day job and relationships will suffer. Did I hear anyone mention the word 'unbalanced'?

So, from the very start, use *Time-Crunched Triathlon* to scribble on, make notes and keep a record of those things that you now no longer have to remember just in your head.

Keeping a Diary

The best habit, used by elite athletes and everyone who wants to be effective at sport, is to use a diary. This can be a simple paper diary. My first diary dates back to 23 September 1985 and still teaches me things to this day. Your diary can be an online system, such as www.trainsmart.com, Garmin Connect, MyTri or ismarttrain. Use whichever suits you best.

Use your diary and *Time-Crunched Triathlon* to log training information, tips and data, and let your mind be free to do what it needs to do for the rest of the day. Another plus is that with your diary you can look back, spot trends, plan better and see how you can get the best from your situation as your training ebbs and flows. Think of your diary like a log-book for a car. And, taking the analogy further, *Time-Crunched Triathlon* is like a manufacturer's manual – only one that is about you and which you'll use time and time again.

Being organized is the key to being a happy and effective triathlete.

Triathlon training alone can consume anything from 300 hours per year, so every single action you do needs to be the most efficient. From finding the running shoe brand/model/serial number that works best or even your online password, to the time of your first 10k personal best (PB) or that great sports masseuse who helped to speed up your recovery from last winter's training – every action needs to be efficient.

So, you've looked through your diary and you've blocked out those times when you're at work, when you're taking the kids to the cinema, when you're meeting your mates for a catch-up once a month, and you've established how much (or how *little*) actual time you have to invest in training and (mostly) what's best to do right now. It's now clear that the optimum way to improve is to become more efficient. Notice that I'm not saying the best way to become better is to do more and more. You're already time-crunched and not a full-time professional, so let's stay in the real world. We can all race each other and sprint-finish at Kona for a sub-8-hour finish time in our dreams. For now we'll deal with reality based on smart coaching. If you've trained to an unhealthy obsessive extent, please turn to Chapter 11 and read that chapter first and foremost. The rest of you come on in ...!

Only Use What is of Use

Triathlon was born out of a healthy desire to explore the boundaries of human possibility. New innovations have always sat very well within the triathlon mentality. Triathlon has fewer restrictive rules, written and unwritten, than most other sports. A sport that grew from an innovative 'could we finish?' mindset embraces a 'could we try?' mentality.

When you're time-crunched, taking a few minutes to organize, plan and review your progress goes a long way to helping you become an effective triathlete.

RIGHT NOW!

Block out 30–60 minutes in your diary every week to review and organize your training. This can mean re-organizing your home-life and training, finding and speaking with training partners, or checking your training diary to see what habits are yet to be ingrained. Do this every week from now on – this weekly 'plan & review' is as vital as the training itself.

This has plusses and minuses: for every great innovation, triathletes have jumped on others that promised much, but which cost money, yet failed to deliver improvement. I hold my hand up (very high) to being caught out a few times, but with 'experimentation' comes experience and new possibilities – which I'm willing to pass on to you here in *Time-Crunched Triathlon*. I have gained from or invented enough innovations to make up for those initial mistakes. It's a balancing act between being an early-adopter and a total sceptic.

So, be sure to use only the technology that fits in with your mindset and that works to make you more efficient. If you're scared of 'complicated', keep things simple. If gadgets motivate you, beware of too much retail therapy!

Always remember that the ultimate reason you buy an item is to make you faster. Even if the gain may be indirect. For example, if you use a Hydrobelt to do deep-water running that improves your run fitness, this could motivate you to swim more often as well. I firmly believe that the odd 'toy' does motivate some people, especially if it is set as a reward for achieving a certain goal, such as buying a new bike when you break your personal best.

However, too many toys can eventually get over-powering. So, just like clothing,

Take a deep-water running belt to the pool and you instantly add time-efficient low-impact running to your sessions.

RIGHT NOW!

Check all the equipment you own and use for training and racing. What's lying unused in a cupboard or box? Are those items already on Santa's Christmas list really necessary? *Really*? Be ruthless! What can you get rid of while making you no less effective as a triathlete? Often, less really is more.

But don't just dump the offending item in the nearest dustbin. You may be able to sell it on eBay and buy something else to make you more effective with the money. You could give it as a gift to motivate a friend in training. Or you could donate it to a local charity shop.

So, pop a reminder into your diary roughly September, January and April each year to 'kit-rationalize'. You'll feel so much better for it.

bikes and electronic gadgets, the tools of your trade must be rationalized occasionally.

Use your **Kit Data** form in Appendix 2 (see page 230) to list what kit you have already and what you might need. Then, if you need to order a piece of kit quickly, you've all the details on hand to bag a bargain and save yourself time and money.

Tech for the Triathlete

As a geek-athlete, I have to admit deep down that I like tech.

There. I've said it. *I like tech.*

The idea of a GPS App to measure

sessions, such as MyTri from www.220Triathlon.com, or uploading data onto iSmartTrain to compare heart rates – or even downloading your InfoCrank Power data to see how well that last interval session went – is all absolutely to be commended. With no hard and fast data, we try to guess or make assumptions based on what we want to hear, not on what the data would have told us. We can all fool ourselves if a bruised ego is the alternative.

Your running shoes won't stay this clean or be effective shock absorbers for ever, so be sure to upgrade before injury strikes.

Granted not every session needs to be downloaded or overly analysed. Just as you don't have to waste ten minutes of running time every session finding a foot pod, or cancel rides if the Garmin is not to hand.

Keep training time greater than 'sat-in-front-of-the-computer' time. Ask yourself – am I addicted to techno gadgets that just make my life more complicated? When I look at my early diaries they were pen and paper with progression and review – very effective, very time-efficient. They weren't perfect, but they did take less time than I see some spend on logging on or overly analysing the icing-on-the-cake instead of being out there baking the cake. And don't ask me why I'm using cooking analogies because I am the world's most incompetent cook – that's official!

Quick Tip

With the steely determination to go through *all* of your equipment, trim down what you have to the optimum amount you need for each session. Reduce any duplication or over-complication like choosing colours.

From open-water swims and Elite ITU racers to pre-race changing and keeping warm at the finish line, innovations like the DryRobe make sense.

Solutions to Finding Time Take Time to Find

The final piece of the puzzle that makes triathlon move from the impossible to the possible is being able to blend training and real life – innovating everyday time slots into training possibilities. So, transform running errands into bike sessions, commutes into steady runs; use a gym near work in your lunch hour – these are all excellent ways to transform a time-slot into a possible 'time-crunched' training opportunity.

As a person ultimately taking part in an event that changes disciplines rapidly, you can also combine different sports – this is not only a good 'transition' training habit, but also time-efficient. For example, a deep-water running (DWR) belt gives you a swim-and-run session that turns the pool into a place to train for running as well. It's a super quick changing-time between the sports and you also get a lower body water-massage thrown in – bonus!

I have found that the slow progress down the pool while deep-water running makes swimming feel fast. It may be a mind trick, but it all helps. Even the simple action of laying kit out the night before an early morning session can prime you to be ready even when you're still bleary-eyed, with no time lost searching for a missing sock or bike helmet.

Here is my top ten time-crunched optimizers, making the difficult much easier for you to achieve:

1   **Add a run to bike rides whenever possible.** Just ten minutes gets your running muscles supporting your body weight and shakes the bike

position 'hunch' out of your posture. It's also a key skill to being a successful triathlete.

2 **Keep a note of the equipment you prefer and know works well for you.** Use the **Kit Data** form within Appendix 2 (see page 230) to list your preferred run shoe model, swim goggle and saddle – plus anything that's a special piece of kit. Then set up an auto search on eBay to get a spare or two at a bargain price, for when you lose it or it breaks.

3 **Keep run shoes and kit in the back of your car.** If time suddenly becomes available on a road-trip or while you're waiting for family/friends, you can squeeze in a cheeky run. (This is also ideal if the car breaks down as you can run to a garage or home!)

4 **Have a turbo trainer set up ready to go or as best as home space allows.** Keep your shoes on the bike and shorts plus cycle top hanging ready nearby. It can always be used before a run to get warmed up for outdoors running.

5 **Run to or from work – or before work and when you get home.** Stealth training by commuting on foot and/or doing a double-run day makes for good time-management and run fitness.

6 **Watch for silly things that cause the most damage.** For example, out of the blue, five-a-side football, over-zealous weight-training, or driving for hours in a hire car without any stretching breaks. Fewer of these hiccups will mean greater training progress for you, so think ahead where possible.

7 **Look at future training-races and check they are time-efficient.** Driving time, the event and post-race nattering all need to be weighed-up against actual race time and the specifics you benefit from (e.g. open-water swimming against others, or riding part of a future A-race course). Especially bear in mind off-season brownie points by simply being around instead of always being elsewhere racing.

Using the turbo trainer is time-efficient – great if you're in a busy built-up area or when you need to stay close to home but wish to gain steady miles or high-intensity intervals.

8 **Have a spare set of road-ready wheels, spare cleats and a chain (with tools).** Then, a session-stopping mechanical can be righted in no time and your plan can continue onwards.

9 **Engage and negotiate with your family about what you're doing in the world of triathlon.** It makes your life so much easier and thus the chances of your success are boosted. We're not doing this alone – that was never the aim of the sport.

10 **Every week do a SWOT of your present actions (see Chapter 2).** Forget your New Year's resolutions — you need to be evolving every week, not once a year! That's 52-times the effect.

Simple recovery meals after training need not take hours or be lacking in quality nutrition.

Make Five-Thirty in the Morning Your Friend

Very few of us like early mornings. In fact, nobody in their right mind likes setting the alarm at silly o'clock. But you have to set your alarm anyway; the time is just a detail. The big bit is setting the alarm. You have to get up before you want to; the rest is all in your mind. So you may as well get something out of it. If you set your alarm for 05.30 a.m., you get a huge amount out of it. In no particular order:

1 **Being up and about when nobody else is:** In spring or summer, cycling with hardly any traffic and beautiful empty mornings ... well, what a way to start! The UK is massively crowded nearly all the time, but far less so at 05.30 a.m.

2 **Get the training out of the way:** This is a guaranteed way to do your training, rather than miss your training due to work/family, etc. Also, a plan is more likely to turn into reality if it is done first

thing and it avoids the 'thinking about it all day' problem, e.g. 'searching for excuses not to go out running' syndrome.

3 **Even long cycle sessions can be completed, leaving almost the rest of the day intact:** A four-hour hard cycle that starts as early as 5.45 a.m. has you home at 9.45 a.m. – barely even mid-morning. Sometimes at the weekend you can be back before your family or partner is even awake. How cool is that?!

4 **Make the most of what time you have:** You will start to think about how early you have to get up, and this makes you go to bed early. This will avoid wasted hours in the evening, like those two hours between 9 p.m. and 11 p.m. Why watch TV when you can go to bed?

5 **Getting used to match conditions:** Finally, for many races (especially Ironman and 70.3) you will be doing the races at these times so you may as well get used to them!

One drawback is that it is hard getting up in the winter. But in January the mornings get lighter each day and from February onwards you should see a real difference and the early starts should not depress you too much. And it is good for the mental training.

Over time, the net effect of starting at 05.30 a.m. is that you take the 90–120 minutes you would usually waste in front of the TV or otherwise the previous evening, and transform these into effective training for the same number of minutes in the morning.

PETER FRASER QC, *four-times Ironman*

One More Thing Before You Go

It's easy for athletes to set great goals (and that's just a few pages away). However, I want to flag up a big warning: a lesson that many of us have already found out; a fact that makes training 'smart' takes on a totally different perspective. Read carefully from here so as not to jump any words. Think 'I know that' and you might jump to your own conclusions ...

The trainability of your genes does not grow as your training frequency,

A smart approach to your training and racing is rewarding, offers a better guarantee of success and brings more happiness in the long run.

volume and intensity increase. In other words, the glass ceiling that your genes have will not always be raised if you just train more often, harder or for more hours per week. We can get you to your peak very quickly, but with little time to learn race-experience, subtly improve efficiency or without a high risk of injury. It is possible to peak quickly, yes. However doing this repeatedly means you will break something: immune system tolerance, motivation or a joint structure that may never fully repair. Ever.

The physical attributes for triathlon are not equally bestowed on all humans. There I've said it, again. At this point someone will leave the room, eBay this book or make my ears burn with a tirade of verbal abuse. Hey, don't shoot the messenger! Often, they have extra useful information if you would only let them complete the message.

Somewhere a potential medal-winner is propping up a bar or enjoying a sport they just find fun – and with no medals to motivate them. Conversely, there are those who train too hard, too quickly in the winter or just too intensely all the time. You want to enjoy the rewards and the journey to get there. Right?

However keen you are to fly through to the end of this chapter so you can stop reading this book and start training, please read below ...

RIGHT NOW!

Think of the possible threats to your continued enjoyment and achievement in triathlon. Be honest and open, but most of all write them in big letters at the back of this book ... today – right now. Threats are our enemies and we need to keep them close, very close to our hearts.

Being Realistic

There are threats to your continued enjoyment of triathlon, the things that could put the whole Project Better-You 3.0 in total jeopardy. So many times I have heard people talk about these things with hindsight. 'I kind-of knew it was wrong, but at the time, you know ....'

If you can keep these threats from happening you can maintain that genetic core. But do some actions wrong repeatedly and you could be starting 10 or 20 per cent further back, with less chance of reaching the 100 per cent you once had. Often athletes think if they start to train more seriously *this year* that suddenly their genes will sprout a 25 per cent improvement. I fully agree all of us must try to get 99 per cent out of our genetic endowment, and that this is not an easy task for anyone to pull off. Yet we should never break ourselves through ignorance of the facts that certain limiters will occur to all of us so we cannot just push to be 110 per cent of the real me or you. Think about this scenario: Miguel Indurain, five-time Tour de France winner, was recently fitness-tested fourteen years after retiring. At his peak he held approximately 497–509 watts for one hour during his record-breaking ride in 1994 – that's probably 1.5–3 times what you might be able to do. His maximal ramp test peak power was 572 watts. Yes – 500 watts for one hour and a maximal of 572 watts in a ramp test. Yet, as he stopped training and aged he was left with a 'mere' 369 watts at his anaerobic threshold and a maximal power of 450 watts. His maximal power had dropped by 122 watts (21.3 per cent) and his anaerobic threshold by 136 watts (505 to 369 watts) or 26.9 per cent decline. At the age of forty-six and relatively untrained, he still showed 'genetic' numbers that I rarely see in all but the very highest level of age-group/semi-professional athlete. No one untrained in their forties has these numbers.

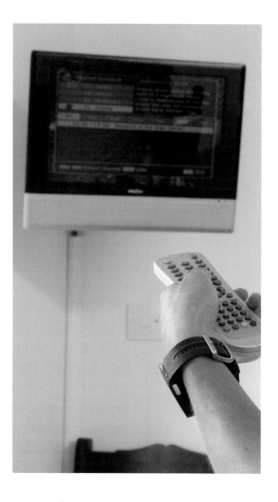

Television is not bad, but it can sap time and leave you angry about missed training or provide you with an excuse to snack too much in the evening, so ration telly time and be a better athlete.

Turn this data around: despite ageing clearly having had an effect over the past fourteen years, Indurain's training 'back in the day' accounts for just 21.6 per cent addition to his world-class engine still visible in his forty-something body. In studies of twins as much as 70–90 per cent of certain physical fitness traits can be down to the underlying genetic framework a person has. Despite trying to push your genes, these internal Darwinian structures really do apply a certain degree of fixed possibilities; a glass ceiling, if you will.

Feeling fit, energetic and knowing that your training is going well can give you a great buzz. Polish your genes carefully but never try to train your Xs and Ys to be something they are not.

HOLIDAYS & TRAINING CAMPS

If your lifestyle allows you to plan a one-, two-, or even three-week summer training holiday, I find that it's best placed so you return home to your normal routine between 2 and 4 weeks before your A-race of the year. This allows you to recover from the hard work with your race form peaking at just the right time. Alternatively, having a week or two in early spring, or near the end of winter, can help kick-start your fitness heading into a new season – this can be good for motivation.

Scott Neyedli, *Ironman UK and Wales winner and full-time worker*

So if you're fairly trained, then your peak is probably far closer than you think, what's the point in trying to hold it too long? Thinking it will go up 20 per cent if you just train 20 per cent harder for 20 per cent more of the yearly cycle is a mistake. A brief flick over the research findings and athlete real-world data on high-intensity interval training suggests that a 4–8 week period of around 40–75 minutes of high-intensity effort per week can add around 5–10 per cent more performance. It's the icing on the cake – and nice icing at that – but it cannot be achieved continuously with 10 per cent every month or quarterly ad infinitum. So when I hear of athletes starting their top-end intervals in November or sounding off about a new interval regime that's the 'secret' of the professionals, I wish we could do one thing. I wish we could write a rule that all high-intensity magazine and online training articles, downloadable programmes and club sessions cite right at the very start:

Remember that high-intensity intervals add the icing on the cake; they don't stop you having to spend hours making the cake in the first place!

The Light that Burns Twice as ...

This is an anonymous story that was always destined to be in a book. Names are not given, but the scenario is real:

> 'I was always keen to ride indoors in the winter. It was good for time-management and meant I got less kit dirty and worn out by the winter. I really enjoyed the sessions, watching videos I had on an old video-player. It was a steady session, but I would sometimes add a sprint when the footage got the better of me. No different to the odd fast jump from traffic lights or nipping onto a mate's back-wheel when you needed to catch up after a stop.
>
> I then got a book that another athlete said helped them for a while on their biking. They didn't say if they used it for swim and run too, but I erred on the side of caution and did it just on the bike. The intervals were hard, but I suppose in January they were always going to be. I definitely lost the mojo to want to go out to the garage to do the intervals, but then that's when I said to myself that others may not be doing this and, as I was doing it, I would surely beat them. If intervals are about

Training must be fun and yet challenging. It never gets any easier to stretch yourself so think long term about your triathlon 'career'.

being hard, then I could prove I was above my 2011 level.

So, jump forward a few months and I was feeling very fit when I looked at my interval sessions. At the first club event I squeezed ahead of a few people that I didn't normally beat, usually, they'd be just ahead of me. I was well on my way to a better season, but didn't let on I had this special book and these intervals – why let them get faster? They were my competition, after all!

Anyway, by the time the proper events started I was ready to do just one or two and then call it a day. I was really tired; I didn't know why – perhaps a virus. It had meant my nearest competitors were starting to beat me. I was back to my usual timings so something wasn't right. I DNS-ed at my main event in August, but got my entry into 2012 transferred. When I look back the season was not what I wanted. It's a shame really because the fitness I showed in March gave me hope that there was a lot more to come if I could stay well and get to the races fit.'

ANON.

After a long explanation to this athlete about their premature form, they did see the error of their ways. The fact that they peaked effectively before the season even started, then just ground themselves down over the following months, meant they were at peak form far too soon, forcing summer fitness at the end of winter. You have a peak – be sure it's there for race-day.

When you race, you feel alive and in the moment. It's the culmination of sweat, toil and sacrifice. Enjoy!

CHAPTER TWO

Goals: Before You Head Outside

You need to look at your current situation and attempt to make small gains each year using training, nutrition and technology while at the same time hanging onto those gains already hard-won. This is a constant, ongoing commitment, or you will go slower next time out. Fitness is fickle. Gains are never banked; they can always be lost through lack of training over time. However, new technology and sports science research have a way of increasing fitness gains. Never underestimate that the passing of time gives you future chances to train, but may also take small amounts away, especially for those of us beyond the 35–40-year age range.

Training with a plan that keeps your enjoyment and rewards high is about making smart choices. Having confidence in your methods is central to being an effective time-crunched athlete.

At a guess, and with plenty of analysis of age-group athletes like you, I think that some people can gain perhaps 10 per cent over a year's worth of very good work. However, they have not already done smart training, brought good equipment or really honed their nutrition. To put it another way: that's a gain of 0.83 per cent per month if such a division could actually happen. This equates to improving the 2-hour 30-minute standard distance triathlete to a 2-hour 15-minute racing snake.

If only the reality were as simple, we could all be great! In fact, in the real world most athletes appear to log gains of 2–5 per cent, on a good year. That's 15 minutes off a 5-hour half Ironman, middle distance and 70.3 event for the 5-hour finisher.

Here's some feedback from Matt Probitts, a triathlete who lamented having to spend his winter training-time more wisely in order to build towards a summer race:

[*early February 2014*] ... in the first month of training with you, I've found that I've seen improvements in all three disciplines. My cycling average speed is the same, but my heart rate is about 20–25 bpm lower. I'm really enjoying training at the moment and the Ironman I've entered is still daunting, but not quite as daunting as it was! I now believe I can complete the race.

[*July 2014*] First, a confession. Up until late January/mid-February, I had real doubts about how 'going slower can make you go faster', but after today I am a true believer!

Now for today's race report. I entered the Thame triathlon late and was in the one of the slower waves. It was a 400 metre swim (in a 25m pool), which took 9 minutes 37 seconds. I would have been quicker. However, I was held up due to slower swimmers in my lane. T1 was good. The bike was exceptional, I felt really good and over-took loads of other competitors, and completed this in 34 minutes 53 seconds. My average speed was a PB at 21.3 miles an hour. T2, again, was good. I pushed hard on the run and managed a pace of 8 minutes 48 seconds per mile, which is pretty good by my standards. I still think I need to improve on my running as this is definitely my weakest discipline.

I had a good race and really enjoyed today. I'm looking forward to Etonman in September. Thank you so much for all your help.

Most experienced triathletes reading this will have several seasons under their belt, and it may be really hard to get within +/-3 per cent of their past performances. We could uncover some missed opportunities to go faster, or be reminded of the 'ergogenics', i.e. those things that can make us faster, which worked previously to speed us up.

The longer it was since this performance, the harder it is to assume that it's a 'given' that you can repeat the effort or take another sneaky 3 per cent off your previous best. Hence my caveat about progression:

There are just as many factors that can make you slower
as there are to make you go faster.

Ergogenics can make you faster, e.g. caffeine. These are countered by ergolytics that will make you slower, e.g. significant gains in body fat.

Those with high-level performances already to their name must search harder each year to find new 'one-percenters' of improvement. However, if they have proved it before when racing, then they do have the ability – courses being equal – to do it again. Experience is still a vital tool on race-day; something that's really hard to quantify, but which shows itself to be invaluable when put to its best use.

However, past gains are not permanent; nor are they guaranteed every year. Significant lifestyle factors may have changed in just twelve months. As a result of ageing, inconsistency, ill-health, equipment failure and so on, you may be struggling just to be near the 'you-on-a-good-day' of three months ago, let alone the 'peak-you' from three years ago. This is made worse if your best was achieved on a short course – your Garmin computer may have told you as such, but perhaps you chose to ignore it. So perhaps you were never quite as fast as you would like to remember? Time is cruel even for the genetically gifted – no one is ever a champion for ever. So, if you want to progress, you must first look at your strengths, weaknesses, opportunities and threats ('SWOT') … and *then* do something about it.

Your equipment is plentiful, even for those trying to be frugal with their investment in the sport. Be organized and savvy as to the best tools for your 'trade'.

Swotting for Success

OK. At the risk of sounding as if we are drifting off into corporate work mode, and I'm about to hit you with a twenty-screen PowerPoint presentation, hear me out. Like Clive Woodward (rugby, athletics), David Brailsford (track cycling, road cycling), and the many other professionals who use their business brains to further improve sport, you too have to be switched on

Learning to relax and unwind at one end of the scale of effort perfectly complements the efforts that training and racing take out of you at the other end of the range.

to the benefits of some analysis of what you do. If you're a training junkie, it's fine to just head out the door and train. I know some love to train at every opportunity and with little planning or logic to their toil. Results? Yes – but laughable in its logic, and not what anyone with a true-goal achievement in mind should do. So, let's leave the training junkies to it, and you and I will sit down and do a little paperwork to extend your lifespan in endurance sports, get the most out of your training, and know when to be 'on-it' or chilling.

First, you must identify your current strengths and weaknesses and gain a clear understanding of what factors help you to train effectively (i.e. opportunities) and what factors put your health, training or racing at risk (i.e. threats).

You can find out this vital knowledge for yourself by drawing up a list of strengths, weaknesses, opportunities and threats.

Let's start by looking at your *strengths* and *weaknesses*. Don't forget to include not only your actual triathlon ability, but also your lifestyle, injury history and psychological make-up.

RIGHT NOW!

For the next 180 seconds – that's three minutes – use the **SWOT** form in Appendix 2 (see pages 211–12) to jot down whatever springs to mind about your strengths and weaknesses. When your three minutes are up, come back here.

Ready, steady ... go!

OK, that was the easy bit. You should now have at least one comment for each category within the sections for strengths and weaknesses on your SWOT form. What you have written will depend on you and your circumstances. You may have written comments like 'My family are very supportive' or 'These days I seem to take longer to recover from minor injuries'. Some categories may have attracted more comments than others. That's fine. You've made a start at looking at where you are right now, and this will help you when you come to work out where to go from here.

Now you need to consider what *opportunities* you have for success and what *threats* there are to achieving that success.

RIGHT NOW!

Go back to the **SWOT** form in Appendix 2 (see pages 213–4) and take another three minutes to jot down whatever springs to mind about what factors help you to train effectively (i.e. opportunities) and what factors put your health, training or racing at risk (i.e. threats).

Again, you should end up with a list of comments, this time identifying any opportunities and threats. Together with the comments you made about your strengths and weaknesses, these comments will help to point you in the right direction and suggest the most appropriate goals for you. However, for now, just put the comments on your strengths and opportunities to one side and let's take a closer look at your *weaknesses* and *threats*.

RIGHT NOW!

Spend another three minutes expanding the comments you made about your weaknesses and threats.

Do you train instead of eat, over-eat after you train, or fail to complement big training days with bigger eating days? All of these scenarios need to be acknowledged in your SWOT.

You have so much to lose if these stack up against you. It's great if you're good at something or if you have four hours a day to train, but I'm more concerned with what limitations and gremlins lurk behind your best side. If you're a food-obsessive or don't like having a rest-day, can't drive, or live miles from a swimming pool, then that is a weakness/threat to be acknowledged. Once you've acknowledged it exists, you can then begin dealing with it effectively.

If I could list those items most likely to damage Project 'Better You', i.e. your 'goal', it would be (in no particular order):

- often training when ill
- building up resentment at home
- running in shoes that should have been replaced months ago
- ignoring body work investment
- unacknowledged shifts in work priorities
- ignoring serious health niggles
- always training to someone else's plan
- never accepting your race times without a caveat
- ignoring advice on equipment set-up
- forgetting that 'shift' happens – so you must be able to change to 'keep-up'
- taking yourself just too damned seriously
- too much Zone 2 training (81–7 per cent HRmax) in so-called steady sessions
- too much Strava ego
- just too much tri, all day, every day, all year round!

Being time-crunched means you take wasted time and plan ahead to transform it into a way of making your training sessions actually happen.

However, before this becomes too negative, let's take another look at all the positives you listed as strengths. These are on your list, so I am guessing that you feel you possess them and they help you. If we work on the right things at the right times, especially our psychology, it's amazing how the programme of training, nutrition and technology will be individually tailored to your specific needs. From observation of needs to logical training sessions – training is geared to help those areas that most need help and keep the good ones permanently good. I guess that's why, as a coach, I am frustrated by training sessions that are neither logical nor tailored to your needs but done because 'other people are doing them'.

But it all starts with that frank, 'warts-and-all' SWOT of you as you are today. So go and get a second opinion on your completed SWOT. Ask your coach or a valued friend. Their response may reveal some home truths and some useful inputs to your list of factors that have significant implications for your achievements as a triathlete. Be brave! It *will* help in the long run.

SIMPLE THINGS HELP LOTS

- Don't leave training to the end of the day – you may miss the opportunity because of circumstances out of your control.
- Get up early! Don't sit there watching television!
- Plan ahead to reduce wasted travel time, so if one day you have to meet with an accountant, shop for food, and squeeze in a swim, try to plan ahead so that you go straight from one to another and not back and forth from home.
- Take your running kit with you everywhere – that way, if you're leaving a meeting in London and the trains are all delayed, you can get changed and go for a run; if you use 'Muck Off' Body wash to freshen up, then spray deodorant, you're fine.
- Take turbo trainer and your bike in your car if you're working away – hotel rooms are great for a cheeky turbo session!
- Have a spare set of swim stuff in the car – again, if a meeting is delayed or traffic is slow, go to nearest pool and do a session rather than waste an hour sitting around in your car.
- If you work with sports-orientated people, have running meetings – these can be highly productive and very time-efficient.

ROGER SHERIDAN, *A/G World Champion qualifier 2012, Lanzarote 70.3 finishes 2015*

Once you have filled in your SWOT form and got a second opinion, transfer all comments from the SWOT form to the **SWOT Analysis** form in Appendix 2 (see page 215).

Even the elites have to undergo a SWOT analysis from time to time. To give you an idea of what your SWOT Analysis form may look like, take a look at the sample SWOT Analysis form completed by multiple Ironman Peter Harding.

Peter Harding's SWOT Analysis form

Activity	Strengths	Weaknesses	Opportunities	Threats
Bike training	Better	Occasional lapses into Zone 2	Better discipline required	Work and time pressure, illness, business
		Time pressure due to commuting	Use of power during training to manage intensity	
Daily diet & sports nutrition usage	Using colostrum, whey protein	Lapses on long distance races have affected results	Better nutritional discipline required for long distance races	Lack of discipline blunts progress
	Proven strategy for losing weight	Weight loss is slow and difficult	Reappraisal of eating habits and weight	
Bike equipment	Good set-up from wind tunnel and multiple seasons racing	Not the most aerodynamic frame or equipment	New TT bike in the wings for 2015	Changes bring uncertainty and instability in performances
Race performance	Consistency, good pacing, great results from last season has improved confidence and underlined what works and what doesn't	Nutrition discipline on long distances (> 5 hour)	Lose weight	Getting older!
			Increase strength and power	
		Hilly courses are a challenge	Optimize equipment	
			Even better pacing and splits	
Work & family commitments	Good support from family		Being freelance gives opportunity and flexibility to train	Work pressure is intense and random, daily commute is time-consuming

You must be realistic. Some of your goals may be difficult to change. For example, a goal of 'long arms improving your stroke length' cannot be achieved by everyone. Certain attributes, though, are just 'you', and these should be permanently written on your SWOT form as a reminder that you have good and bad attributes. You can and will transform certain parts of your SWOT profile over time. So keep that completed SWOT form and SWOT Analysis form handy, and update them over time.

But right now your SWOT analysis can point to some quick gains for little or no effort – what we call 'low-lying fruit'.

Actions Start with a SWOT

OK, now you need to take a more detailed look at your SWOT analysis form so that you can identify what you can turn into solid actions over the longer term. Taking the comments on your SWOT Analysis form and transforming them into actions is key to becoming a smarter, time-crunched triathlete.

Overleaf follows an example of Peter Harding's earlier SWOT analysis form, but now with actions added.

Action gets SWOTs looking better over time; SWOTs *never* get better by simply hoping that things will turn out for the best. You can't just have the idea that you'd like to do something about your weaknesses or threats – you really must put your plan into action.

Start a Plan

Quick Tip

Get some immediate 'low-lying fruit' by taking some easy, instant actions on weaknesses or threats, such as replacing old running shoes or warming up slowly before you meet up with a group of training friends who always seem to go off too fast.

RIGHT NOW!

Take a closer look at your completed SWOT analysis form and list 3–6 tasks you need to complete before the end of the week. List each task on a sheet of A4 or in your training diary or on a note stuck to the fridge door. Then, as you complete each task, tick or cross it off, and feel smug as you gain control.

The bones of your weekly training plan come from seeing which sport you must plan to happen, or it gets forgotten or becomes the current weaklink. The training sessions or order of sessions in the next seven days will differ from those in six months' time. A week's plan must constantly take into account past training and the upcoming week.

Your plan is a starting point and, while you may not get it all done, you can ensure effort goes into those things most likely to give you positive

Peter Harding's SWOT Analysis form with actions

Discipline	Last Race (previous)	Areas for Improvement	Strategy Goal	Goal	Action
Swim	1:19 (1:26)	Endurance and efficiency	More winter swim metres = 1:50/100 metres	1:15	Swim sessions with a group Strength & endurance weights Technique focus in winter
T1	5:11 (8:??)			5:00	
Bike	6:11 (7:11)	Further improvement in leg endurance and strength Use of time trials or group rides for hard workouts in-season	Structured programme to build on new endurance Winter consistency = 18–19 mph	6:00	Link up with stronger riders HR targets Feeding strategy Winter training in- and/or outdoor Long bikes in-season Interval work >Feb Strength training?
T2	?:??? (???)	?	Bricks	5:00	Bricks with timed T2
Run	2:11:11 (20.5k)	Keeping going through second half Sustain easy first 10 km pace at 1:05 through the rest of the marathon	Structured run programme 10:30/mile	4:30	Build long-run time to 3:00 Interval work (controlled) Bricks with race feeding beforehand Injury management
Nutrition & Body Work		Bike nutrition Work on lower back massage/physio Corrective action to bike set up	Do all three ahead of training		Sort stomach problem (colostrum 2–3 months) Get regular off-season massage Get bike photographs done and email them to coach
Overall	DNF vs FINISH	Need to go sub 12 (but finish first and foremost)		11:5 5:00	

RIGHT NOW!

Make a weekly plan that is effective and relevant and based on recent training events, not the best week ever. Aim to build a solid series of bricks in the training-wall.

Having a training diary online is not an excuse to surf the web for hours or lose sleep over-analysing the simplest of sessions. Planning, logging and reviewing should not take hours on end.

performance gains, not just short-term ego massaging or beating a racing rival during training. We all love certain sessions, but no one session or sport can train you for the three entirely different movement patterns of swim, bike and run. As a triathlete, you are a jack of all trades – you must train for all of those trades.

Get a Weekly Reality Nudge

The very best way to evolve as a time-crunched triathlete is constantly to return to your present reality, i.e. your SWOT, to check that it's on track to making you what you want to become, i.e. the 'Better You'. Anything not achieved one week either rolls on to the next week, or is superseded by another, more important, task. Be clear that an impossible goal is not suddenly possible to achieve just because you have a plan.

There are many who make impossible goals because it means they can be a valiant trier when they eventually fail. Wrong! That's just deluding yourself and is a waste of time. Your evolution from what you are right now is a subtle and, ultimately, finite process. We cannot (despite lots of empowerment books and audio) – repeat: *cannot* – all jump over the moon ...

RIGHT NOW!

Put a monthly reminder in your diary, smartphone or wall planner to update your SWOT – and possibly your goal(s), too.

even if the cow in the nursery rhyme did manage this. (*Note:* witnesses of Cat, Fiddle, Little Dog, Dish and Spoon may not be 100 per cent reliable.)

I'm deliberately not forcing you to complete tons of paperwork. I don't want to turn athletes into admin assistants. This process should take no more than a few minutes each week, in addition to filling in your training diary and planning your week ('synchronize diaries, everybody!'). Ultimately, this approach *reduces* the paperwork littering your life: from that nagging little yellow Post-It note stuck to your turbo trainer to those random 'get-it-off-your-chest' lists at the back of an office diary.

The best athletes are organized, not headless; mindful toilers – not mindless masochists. Ever wondered why the elites can tell you most days what they are doing, what their rep times are (and so on)? It's because they are engaged in the development of their weekly plan: an evolving plan – not just a 'copy-a-friend' format. They know what they are doing because they have sought the best way to do things, for their livelihood. This shouldn't eliminate fun, spontaneity or the chance to blend in other people's ideas. It's a tried and tested, but flexible, framework that empowers your actions and saves you having to try to remember too many things in your head. Simple but effective.

Training efficiently and to your goals does not mean being a monk. Join other people's sessions, have mini-races – but know what you to have achieve by the week's end.

You may be tempted to skip to Chapter 7 to pick up some nutrition tweaks, or re-visit the 'beat winter' tips in Chapter 9. Perhaps buying performance most appeals to you and so you're itching to read Chapter 8? I strongly urge you not to! Stick with this chapter; absorb its advice, then

follow it. Whatever else you take from this book, the most important elements can be found here within this chapter. Everything else in the book flows from this. All your actions must be relevant to your SWOT, or any action brought about by information elsewhere (from within this book – or anywhere else in the universe, for that matter) is just a distraction to keep you occupied, but will not help you become the 'Better You'. Sometimes goals, plans or actions are more about being able to step back and maintain focus and balance ...

FIVE WAYS TO BALANCE IT ALL

1 **It's common sense, but organization is key:** work out your key sessions and try to get them in as a priority. Then check to see when the most likely point in each week exists that could accommodate these sessions – everything else on top is a bonus!

2 **Use your commute time if at all possible:** Then use this as 'absolutely a time to think about work' or 'absolutely a time *not* to think about work' – you then get to use the time more efficiently. I do loads of work stuff in my head when I'm running as I don't get interrupted.

3 **Pre-negotiate your holiday with your other half:** Before you go, work out if it's a no-training holiday or, even better, a race at the start of the holiday, followed by a non-training holiday. For example, I entered Mallorca 70.3 for three years on the trot whereby I'd do the race, then we as a family would have a week's holiday in Mallorca where I do absolutely no training at all. This worked well for all of us as a family.

4 **Recognize that even a twenty-minute run is better than nothing:** I still find this hard to do as twenty minutes isn't long and feels a bit like a waste of time – but it all adds up.

5 **Improve your nutrition:** my major weakness of 'what', 'when' and 'how much' you eat doesn't really take any time at all, but can make a huge difference to race performance. Anybody can get better at their nutrition regardless of how busy they are. This is easy to say and difficult to always do when you're really busy and stressed about work and family life, etc.

If you really want to find some time, you can find some time – just maybe not as much or always when you really want it.

PETE ROBINS, *Dad, director and damned-fine sub-5-hour Ironman 70.3 racer*

It's Not Your Goal But It's Illuminating …

If you want to see how an athlete can manage to shoehorn training into their lifestyle while others rush home to watch 'Corrie' with yet another pizza (or sit on a beach for a week), here's Scott Neyedli's typical training around work. This is not the goal for every triathlete reading this. Scott has no kids, but he is highly motivated and can win big races off this dedicated training, so the sacrifices are worth his effort. Over to Scott …

Commute runs for all or part of the way to and from work are great stealth training and often give a clarity of thought that driving or public transport does not.

Balancing Tri with Life

A lot of my key or focused sessions were in the evening after work and then overload longer bikes at the weekends. I would eat a snack and have a protein shake in between double sessions in the evenings, returning home about 9:30–10 p.m.; have dinner, bath and bed.

Monday
day off: may cycle to and from work (easy!)
sports massage evening

Tuesday
cycle to and from work
then two hours' group ride – intense chain-gang session with run of 40–90 minutes off the bike

Wednesday
run to and from work
masters' swim squad evening

Thursday

cycle to and from work

then two hours' group ride – intense chain-gang session with brick run of 10–20 minutes

followed by masters' swim squad

Evening

1–2 hours run repeats with running club (extra time added from 1–2 hours if Ironman key training)

followed by masters' swim squad evening

Friday

cycle to and from work

run off bike after getting home for 60–120 minutes

Saturday

morning: masters' swim squad

afternoon: bike 2–3 hour fartlek hilly lumpy route on my own + maybe 10-minute run afterwards

early evening: run 40–90 minutes hilly

Sunday

morning: group ride 3–5hrs – may do extra time on top; add brick run 20–40 minutes

late afternoon: recovery swim solo – Hungarian (pyramid) 1500 metre mix paddles, pull & swim (4.6K) or 3K repeats set

… and back round to another Monday rest day.

SCOTT NEYEDLI, *Ironman Wales Champion 2013, National Middle Distance Champion 2013, and full-time worker*

Keep an eye on time so that you start your session with an updated and realistic objective that is achievable.

During the key summer phase of training before his amazing Ironman Wales win in 2013, Scott Neyedli clocked 84 hours in 18 days of holiday taken in Canada (14 June 2013 to 1 July 2013). One particular week included 38 hours of training (swim 4 hours, cycle 23 hours, run 11 hours). A typical at-home training week is 16–20 hours. Yet, before winning the 2013 Middle Distance Championships on 8 June 2013, Scott did just 4.5 hours of training in the five-day taper (swim 1 hour, bike 2 hours 45 minutes, run 35 minutes) up to the event.

This illustrates:

1 Very large volume training blocks require time off work to be absorbed – and for most amateurs that's not a realistic task to attempt.
2 Tapering off training as you approach an event gives you the chance to give your best effort on race day.
3 Even when you've completed – or even won – an Ironman, before you have to go back to the work grindstone, next time you'll be able to give it your best effort.

CHAPTER THREE

Avoiding the Pitfalls

Less time equals more effort – or it is according to the logic of many of the sessions organized by clubs, or groups of friends, or those solo training sessions where many triathletes are left to their own devices or hang-ups. The philosophy, pure and simple, is always to insert some sort of speed work, to finish the session tired, and it's junk if you're not doing as much as can be rammed into the available time. Yes?

No! Less time actually means having to be more effective. That's what you'll learn to do here.

First Rule of Fit Club: Around 80 per cent of Training is Easy

The best way to improve at endurance exercise is to perform at least 75 per cent to as much as 90 per cent of your training at an easy-to-moderate level of exertion.

For the purists, geeks and those of you looking to find caveats, the easy-to-moderate exertion zone is 55–80 per cent of your maximum heart rate.

Training with friends can keep you in the right steady zone for the majority of your training time. Be flexible and chill if it feels too easy – if everyone is smiling, it's likely to happen week after week.

The Biggest Pitfall

So that's the science condensed into thirty-four words (see 'First Rule of Fit Club', above).

Yet, the biggest pitfall for you as a time-crunched or self-coached triathlete is believing that you must always be pushing session output upwards. But think again. By that logic, if you ran six miles in one hour last week, then this week you must run at least 6.5 miles in the same time. And the week following you must run even faster – and every week after. However, observation of effective athletes' training diaries, HR data and/ or lactate levels, plus numerous controlled training studies, all prove that pushing the fastest pace for most sessions is the *wrong* training effort to use predominantly. Training in this 'ego' training zone feels like it's hard enough to get a workout tiredness effect, and it can be sustained for quite long periods, but it's *not* the most effective way forward.

You know the scenario: a steady group run, a three-minute warm-up, then as fast as the next person is going ... until you finish. Or the ride that never lets you catch your breath; someone always pushing the pace to aim for a particular average speed or the next Strava segment! Perhaps a swim where you're panting at the end of the first fifty and for most of the session you're unable to chat during recoveries because you're always trying to get your breath back. So, join the effective triathlete training programme today by easing up on most sessions. This is your licence not only to make most sessions steady, easy and enjoyable, but also properly A-E-R-O-B-I-C. Check out the **Heart Rate Training Zones** form in Appendix 2 (see page 216) – even if you're an experienced athlete, HR does change subtly over time and it's worth keeping up to date. Perhaps you really should get a maximum HR test (drop all other complicated data you can be bamboozled by) and then work off true data from now, not yesteryear? It's your call.

Why does this training work? Well, if you keep below 80 per cent of your maximum heart rate, you keep oxygen delivery adequate. Amongst other things, this keeps lactate – a by-product of insufficient oxygen delivery – down to tolerable levels, which means less stress on your body. However, despite the sceptics, you still get a great deal of aerobic training benefit with little detrimental physiological stress. Also, this approach allows you time to focus on good technique while allowing warm-ups and cool-downs to be considered as training time and not junk. Most importantly, it encourages you to go easy between short-run intervals, hill-climb biking efforts or swim lactate-tolerance sets in the pool. This is not wasted time between hard intervals, but valuable recovery time and, as such, is a vital element of your training session.

The science of triathlon shows the simple truth:

You either go easy (most of the time) or hard (in planned high-intensity sessions), but rarely in 'no-man's land' where you most commonly compete.

Swimming drills side by side (when lane space allows) are a great way to keep it easy and fun. Just don't turn it into a race.

I know that it's essential to know how fast you go when you go hard for short durations in interval efforts or time trials. It's the reality of how much peak racing ability you truly have. At a certain HR you go above your ability to maintain effort aerobically – that is, you surpass your anaerobic threshold, and lactate starts to build. Going hard gets harder and harder to cling to.

This happens around 83–91 per cent of your maximum HR, depending on how fit you are. You have limited time in this area; you cannot continue in this red zone (Zone 3) because your energy use is exceeding your ability to make your muscles contract aerobically. You build up lactate (and other less than useful by-products), and the only way to clear this is to slow down and 're-pay' the lactate overdraft with an oxygen infusion to fatiguing cells.

The important line dividing easy, 'proper', endurance-zone training and 'too-hard-to-be-called-steady' training is the '80 per cent of a person's maximum heart rate' point. Please be clear: this is not *my* own personal zones division that I have invented in an attempt to take over endurance training methods or have some Best Endurance Effort Rating Zone (BEERZ) acronym to live long after me. Nope, this three-zone definition has been devised by sports scientists across the globe, using data from across the gene pool of the human race:

Zone 1 below 80 per cent of maximum heart rate and ideally 60–75 per cent of maximum heart rate represents low stress but good aerobic training; time possible in this zone is many minutes to many hours.

Zone 2 this zone sits precariously just above Zone 1, yet can be done for extended periods – it is easier than the proper hard training 'Red Zone Three'.

Zone 3 above 87 per cent of maximum heart rate and ideally below 93 per cent of maximum heart rate is a high stress zone that represents quality work, i.e. proper 'hard' for proper quality work; time possible here is divided into intervals with rest, e.g. four to six intervals of 4-minutes hard work with 3 to 5 minutes of recovery between.

Granted Zone 1 doesn't do what Zone 3 hard intervals can do, but endurance training is the cake and the intervals are the icing. *Geddit?*

So, you may have done a maximal test or via YouTube seen someone doing a max test (see http://bit.ly/Vid460wMAX). This super-hard effort will find your ceiling heart rate, i.e. the maximum beats per minute that your ticker is pushed by your exercising muscles. You then simply multiply this number by 0.8. Ignore VO_2max tests (this is the maximum volume of oxygen your body can process in one minute) or the ten pages of stats you can be thrown when doing some maximal test services. For example, a score of 185 max gives you an 80 per cent ceiling limit at the top of Zone 1 of 148.

Similarly, you can also take the average heart rate (HR) you've held for a 20–30 minute maximal racing effort (such as a 5–8k run or 20 kilometre bike). This is then divided by 0.9 to give another approximate maximum heart rate – then multiplied by 0.8 to get aerobic ceiling limit of Zone 1. Eventually, with several sources of HR data your zones will be approximated more accurately. If you don't want to use HR all the time (which no one should) I have a surprise for you ....

RIGHT NOW!

Go to the **Heart Rate Training Zones** form in Appendix 2 (see page 216) and start filling in data for your bike and run. Few people use heart rate (HR) during swimming to define their training. I believe that it's possible to use the perception of effort honed over time in cycle and run to use for swimming (or other sports).

Go Low Tech and Ego-Free

When time is limited and you really don't want to be wasting what time you do have looking for a heart rate monitor (or perhaps you just like low-tech?), try this no-electronics-, no-batteries-required option to gauge your training.

During the next week's bike and run training, occasionally keep your mouth shut and use your nose, not your mouth, to breathe: both in and out through the nostrils only. You can also glance at an HR monitor to see what HR limits this tends to keep you within. I grant you that it may well slow you down, especially when running. But stick to it: it's probably the simplest tool for making Zone 1 training a relaxed, effective training habit.

This nose-breathing is nearly always available to you and holds your HR below 80 per cent of maximum. This is your *smart breathing habit*. If you have a cold and can't nose-breathe through congested nasal passages, granted it may not work! However, I would argue if you're that unwell, you probably won't benefit from training in any case. If you're well but simply 'cannot train that slow' (as one athlete put it), then sorry but you have to mentally get your head around slowing down in your 'base' endurance training.

A heart rate monitor really does let you look inside and see how hard your endurance engine is working. Hard intervals, recoveries or steady state – it tells you how hard you are working.

Some pretend they are nose-breathing while clearly going too fast. You can always tell as they heave their chest up and down and snort like an angry bull having just found out its new address is Pamplona. That's not nose-breathing; that's excessive, definitely *un*-relaxed 'effort' channelled through the nostrils.

Restricting your breathing this way will challenge you if you are more used to keeping up with others in what *should* be 'steady' sessions but which are clearly not. In truth, such sessions are more like racing-in-training to survive at someone else's speed. Put very simply:

> *If you can't nose-breathe and it's an endurance*
> *or technique session, you're training all wrong.*

The Hare and the Tortoise – Again

I like to have athletes run a simple fitness test. I have them warm up with easy jogging for 10–15 minutes, chatting between themselves and keeping HR (and ego) under control. Then it's four laps of a 400 m track, starting at the line 9.3 metres back from the finishing line, just to be sure that we do a clear mile (4 × 400 metres + 9.334 metres = 1 mile).

Picture the scenario: it's a February training camp at Club La Santa, Lanzarote. Forty-one athletes are listening to my instructions having completed the warm-up. They are all now told to nose-breathe only and to keep their mouths closed. The key is to run one mile while breathing through the nose so as to get an aerobic mile time, keeping just below 80 per cent of each athlete's maximum heart rate.

The runners set off. Immediately, as one would expect, faster runners pull away from those slower. Around 75 seconds later the first few pass the one-lap point. These are the faster runners; they are still nose-breathing; after them come the rest of the group, one by one – all nose-breathing, as instructed.

Brilliant! This is working!

However, there are always some runners who can't swallow their pride. They are managing to exceed their nose-breathing level *and* they can pass me and another helper while doing so.

However, I am wise to these athletes. I am wise to the fact that cheats exist. Even more, that these cheats are cheating themselves, not the test. It's their test, after all. It doesn't mean anything to me who crosses the finishing line first – because there is no winner here. It's a reality check, not a race.

So, before the runners start, two helpers position themselves on the far side of the track – to all intents and purposes looking as if they are whispering sweet nothings to one another and ignoring the runners; they are just innocent bystanders, oblivious to the effort playing out on the track beside them. No, not really …

Actually, they are my aerobic-training spies, spotting the runners who aren't nose-breathing and who are gasping for breath away from my gaze. Two hundred metres away from my gaze.

When the run is over, the fastest nose-breathing milers turn out to be the fastest 10k runners. A timing of 4:59 for an aerobic mile has been achieved by an age-group World Duathlon Champion and a 31-minute 10k runner. The slowest have taken 10 minutes and were 60-minute 10k runners. Amazingly, the test has demonstrated who should race fastest, yet their effort was (for all bar the cheaters) kept at or below 80 per cent of their maximum heart rate.

However, when my 'spies' wandered over, they confirmed my suspicions: the runners who seemed to be running above their actual aerobic ability were not, in fact, aerobic. Out of view, these runners were breathing hard and through the mouth. And by this, they had turned an aerobic test into an anaerobic race. We hadn't put numbers on with race dots. We hadn't declared this to be a one-mile race. There were no results, no winners. Yet these runners could not let other more aerobically fit people 'beat' them.

The upshot of this was the slower runners got a valid aerobic mile, as did everyone bar one. This is useful because it was a flat surface with no excessive wind and only modest temperatures: this would be the fastest aerobic pace any of the group should expect to run their endurance training at. This aerobic-mile test can be repeated, at little cost in time or effort, and each person gets a measure on their aerobic fitness and efficiency.

Sadly, our cheats proved, alongside other sessions noted by my helpers, that these persons competed 'all of the time'. Without fail. Pointless effort when training is for *your* physiology, not someone else's. It's especially pointless if you try this stunt up against an age-group elite. Or a pure elite. I wish I could also say this was the only time it happened, and only during the aerobic-mile test. I would be lying. Some will never get training smart.

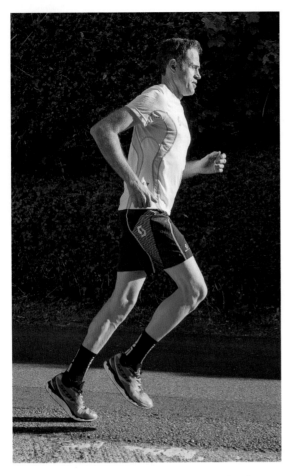

Running aerobically is not racing – it's running aerobically. Relax and enjoy the view. If it's not a hard session, save mental energy for when it is.

Quick Tip

Limit time in front of the TV to the programmes you really, really want to watch. Don't let it affect your sleep or distract you from good recovery, good nutrition and good relaxation.

If this story rings a bell to you, remember:

If you're not part of the solution,
you're part of the problem.

Problem or Solution?

If you're not part of the solution to training smart, i.e. using the Zone 1 habit during most of your training, then you're part of the problem. If you constantly push others in sessions that are not races, you're a junk-trainer. It's an epidemic: training too fast on steady sessions and not hard enough on the quality work. If you're interested in the science of why, see http://bit.ly/1Fppqsm, but remember that most training sessions are not to be pushed hard: only a few per week can be hard 'efforts' (1–3 per week at the last scientific 'guesstimate').

The rest is cruising, albeit sometimes tired, sore or in a grump. Or with meticulous attention to every hand placement, foot action or head movement. The emphasis more often than not has to be on good form, not more muscular effort. So sessions can feel a bit of an effort, but the actual energy expended is on cruise mode.

Lee Piercy is a highly talented athlete, hard-working in his sport and career; yet he's not afraid to miss sessions if they don't work for him and, instead, find a session that works or a training-partner who does know what they are doing. When you have limited time for your sport, what is the point in doing someone else's training all the time? Hard sessions are dealt with in Chapter 5. For now, focus on cruising, at *your* cruise pace, and read the rest of this chapter to help quell the other pitfalls of the time-crunched athlete.

Quick Tip

I have followed the advice, including heart rate, and gone from 15 mph to an 18 mph Ironman Kalmar at the weekend. I entered it to complete it, but all this smart training had me finish in 13 hours enjoying every minute when last year it seemed impossible. Hooked on your [Joe Beer] podcast will keep listening to hit my speed goals. Now #anythingispossible.
DAWN 'DESRIDER', *iTunes review published 19 August 2014*

Top triathletes like Vicky Gill came into the sport with great credentials. We can't all do a minimum nine-hour Ironman or stand on elite-level podiums. But we can certainly learn from these athletes' effective training methods.

RIGHT NOW!

Grab a highlighter (or be prepared to colour/highlight it if it's an online diary) and colour the sessions that got out of hand, that ended up being nothing like you planned them, or that involved random efforts you or someone else inserted 'off-plan'. It could be you chose the wrong course, tried a different group session, or even partnered with someone who had an agenda to make a race out of a session you entered thinking it was training. At this stage, that doesn't matter; what does matter is identifying that particular session as being not quite 'optimal'.

Quick Tip

If you want to train easy or specific, don't train in a group unless everyone has agreed to comply with your training goals. The danger is that you will convert an easy session into something harder and jeopardize your own training.

LEE PIERCY, *Powerman Arizona 2015 winner, multiple Age Group National, European and World Champion Duathlete*

Take ten minutes out from this chapter to look at your training over the past month. Be brutally honest. This is when it truly is a case of 'no pain, no gain'.

Now you should look at the balance of training. Are there some fun efforts but mainly on plan? A bit sporadic? Or just plain race-race-race everything and everybody? Be honest because if you're racing when you pretend you're just cruising, your training will be sub-standard and you won't get the best out of it. It's not too late to change, but you need to acknowledge your problem first and foremost. Join the club – Anaerobics Anonymous has plenty of other Zone 2 junkies keen to drag you down into their thinking.

Training hard is an addictive drug that seems to fit with some people's warped logic that training cannot be easy *and* effective at the same time. The bottom-line is:

Is your 'planning' ahead of time anything like your actual 'actions' in reality?

If not, something needs to change – it's up to you.

Sad Fact But True

I like to get research from journals, look at the findings, the methods and consider 'how does this change the training and racing model?' Friends – yes, *friends* – say that I'm both a geek and a boffin. I'm happy with that and like to think there's a useful outcome for athletes like yourself from this study of endurance training.

For example, I understand the bigger picture so you can be given only the necessary relevant details. A 'need-to-know' basis, if you like.

The simple explanation of why base training works well is probably that it keeps stress low, and movement patterns focused and efficient. Top experts, like Stephen Seiler, suggest that base training keeps the autonomic system stressed less, allowing recovery to take place while also allowing top-quality intervals to take place.

Most of all, Zone 1 training can be reproduced time and time again. The studies, scientists and sports experts in multiple endurance sports show that 60–80 per cent of HR max is actually enough stimulus to create a positive aerobic training session. Whoever you are.

Hence, when you know that low- to moderate-level training has huge benefits, it is surprising to hear these statements from athletes:

- 'I have to train at an average speed of 20 mph on the bike.'
- 'I cannot train that slow; it's junk training.'
- 'That's OK for elites – they have all day to train.'
- 'If I train with fast people I think I might get fast.'
- 'I've been able to train in Zone 2 for ages so how can it be bad?'

Instead, these statements should be:

- 'I train at 120 to 150 beats and my average depends on the course, which bike I use and what time of year it is. I feel really fit and motivated at present.'
- 'Junk training is not warming up slowly enough, exceeding Zone 1 to beat other people, or just plain training when extremely fatigued. I'm bored with Zone 2 junkies.'
- 'If elites could do it in an hour and rest twenty-three hours, then they would. I need to factor in what training I can do and how best to recover with other priorities in my life. My kids don't shut down if I'm too exhausted from training.'
- 'If I train with fast people they will be cruising and I will be racing. That's okay if I want to be flat out and use other people to keep me going fast – but I'm certainly not doing that every week!'
- 'Zone 2 is left for race-day, pace judgement and building up to Zone 3 when I need to add speed. It's tempo training that I use sparingly.'

Do most of your training sessions with people who respect you and know what they are doing. Leave the competitive sessions with 'opponents' for when you really want to race.

Second Rule of Fit Club: #nevergetcold

I hope you're ready. The second rule of fit club is about being warm, not macho. Properly dressed, not under-prepared. Unless you truly are training for Iceman or Arctic triathlons, it's about being optimal with clothing, not minimal. Granted, I get the idea of battling the weather by running through sleet or heading out on the bike for two hours knowing that you're going to be hammered by the rain. It can be good for the soul, and still gives me a buzz when stood in the shower after such a session while trying to get rid of the chilblains.

Yet, I would never attempt these winter sessions in a tri-suit or with the same clothing as a mid-summer session. Know this, and know it well: if you get too cold – guess what? – you over-exert to stay warm and more often than not end up breaking the first rule of fit club (see page 45 for a refresher). Like all good rules, they are symbiotic.

Muscles have greater inefficiencies, and internal effort is wasted when cold. You need to get rid of heat as you make it, hence clothing must be layered and made of suitable materials. If you start too cold (or stop mid-session, then get cold due to lack of additional layers), you're breaking rule two: never get cold.

Watch professional athletes as they come out to train/perform. You'll see them keep themselves warm with exercises and remove or add layers depending on the length of training, plus they don't worry about putting on extra clothing. And that's not just because it means they have even more logo space for sponsors!

The second rule is counter to the mindset that 'tri', 'iron' and 'endurance' are part of triathlon so we're all so hard the weather is irrelevant. You're hard, tough, know no-limits. But keeping your working muscles warm most of the time is central to good endurance training. Research data from even a minor cooling-off period between warm-up and maximal sprinting shows that the athlete who keeps warm out-performs the one left to lose heat and who cools down while wearing insufficient clothing. I'm not saying that you must add heated trousers to your kit list, but they are already being used by top cyclists in track racing to keep muscles operating at an optimal temperature. The shell suit could make a come-back yet.

My experience when cycling, running, doing triathlon and just about every other endurance sport shows that elites (and smart amateurs) keep warm when they could otherwise get cold. Being part of the elite doesn't mean they are immune to the cold or that they possess a special type of muscle that beats good clothing choices and routines. Here are some examples of good (and bad) clothing decisions:

After your usual warm-up routine, keeping yourself warm before a race comes down to two things: putting on your DryRobe and keeping your feet dry.

- Elite runners in Bushey Park seen in full shell suits running past a gaggle of age-group triathletes who were stood around comfortably wearing T-shirts and shorts (at the ready for a start-stop photo-shoot). It was a lovely day in May.
- UCI pro-team riders in full 'longs' and 'Roubaix tops' (that's full tights and thick tops to me and you) with temperatures in the mid-teens. Most amateurs have just shorts on at this point.
- Elite UK triathletes at the London Grand Final 2012 wearing full-length 'keep warm' parka-style jackets supplied by DryRobe right until the moment they walked along the start pontoon. This was tweeted soon after with a pic so I know this is now global and no inside secret.
- Anyone having ever watched swim meets or track-and-field on TV can see the competitors taking off layers, having warmed up out of sight for a great deal of time.
- A top time triallist and sometime triathlete Blake Pond once commented to me: 'Below twenty degrees, don't show your knees' – yet I see less experienced riders in five degrees in shorts!'

So remember to warm up and replace or keep layers on to keep the muscles warm, then compete in the right amount of clothing.

Many, many times, age-groupers complain about below-par performances that coincide with them getting cold before the start of a race. Standing around on wet ground before triathlons or getting wet, then suffering delays in cycle/run races, are the typical worst-case scenarios.

OK – so, in very hot weather you may be looking to try to cool down fast during or after training or racing. Possibly, you may like to pre-cool to reduce your core temperature levels before you race.

Some techniques for this involve:

- wearing bright-white, thin lycra clothing to reflect heat and allow optimal sweating
- soaking your hands in cold water or carrying ice cubes beneath forearm sweat bands
- pouring cold water over your head
- drinking a cold 'slush puppy' energy drink

Steady-run training may cause more heat build-up than cycling outdoors, but you should avoid uncovering your legs and upper body unless it's at least 12–15°C.

It is rare to have to worry about keeping cool. Tri-suits, arm coolers and compression socks can all reduce bare skin on show and increase areas from which heat might be reflected. In February 2014, one client of mine who was racing in the Geelong 70.3 in Victoria, Australia, wore heat- and light-reflective clothing far different to another of my clients based in the UK, who was experiencing zero to 10°C temperatures in a sportive. Obvious? Well, both athletes concerned were UK-born and had been to the UK in the previous year, yet needed vastly different clothing as they were worn 12,000 miles apart. Most UK training sessions outside the season have cool to cold periods, but in race season it is still rare to get temperatures above 25°C. Often, racing is over long before peak tempera-tures are experienced. More likely, you will find that while the race season is on, the temperature is cool enough to chill during early morning sessions, especially if you stand around in Lycra only. In these situ-ations, keeping warm, not cooling down, is more pertinent. Even clients in Australia, Spain and France still complain about rainy or cold mornings (though fewer complain than UK athletes – a lot fewer).

By wrapping up correctly you ensure that you don't cause internal stress on your joints – this gives your working muscles the optimum blood flow for correct fuel use. Cold muscles do not have either good neural coordination or muscle-efficiency. Athletes who start cold *always* have to force the pace to get warm and stay warm.

> ## RIGHT NOW!
>
> Take five minutes to think about your typical clothing choices for sessions over the past week. Do you tend to wear much less than other people? Or do you get it about right? Seasons and the weather within each season can vary hugely – does your training attire adjust or always stay the same? Think, then adapt as necessary.

Third Rule of Fit Club: Warm Up!

If you want to stress your body and make your base training diligence produce less reward, then start your sessions too hard. From the swimmer whose first two lengths are their fastest, the biker who hits a hard hill immediately they start pedalling, and the runner who clicks their stop-watch and cranks up to speed 50 metres out of their front door – I've seen and had to undo many a poor warm-up habit. If you want to get a session wrong, start too hard. Much like if you want to make racing unduly diffi-cult and slower, hit the maximum race pace you may be able to tolerate too early.

I can only think that our evolution demanded one of two things from our ancestors, from whom we get many of our genes and traits:

1. Sprint really hard because something has pounced on you and you need to run away or you die. Sprinting here involves a very brief effort for maximum results: survive or get eaten!

2 Trek at slow speed to stalk an animal, or gather plants that would not run away from you. This approach ensured you had a good chance of getting food energy as you expend muscular energy.

We didn't rush out of the cave at top speed, maintaining this pace for one, two or more hours to find food (whether animal or vegetable). That would have been energetically inefficient and would have meant another less smart species rising to the top of the food chain. So, use your brain: start sessions slow, with a gradual warm-up.

Why Bother? It's Junk Time!

When you warm up, you're moving your inner metabolism from being at your desk, juggling kids or driving to your gym/club session into the high-energy-burning endurance world. If you are sitting down while reading this, you are at present using about one calorie per kilogram of your body weight per hour as you read. So, let's say 55–90 calories per hour covers most readers (i.e. 55–90 kilograms). Assuming that you start running at an easy pace of 10–12 minutes per mile, this equates to around 400–800 calories per hour being demanded by your muscles – the higher figure for the heavier athletes. That's at least a six- to eightfold increase in energy demand, which must be met by using the best fuel stored in the muscle for fast energy conversion, i.e. glycogen (carbohydrate). The harder the blast-off at the start of the session, the greater this glycogen is dented and, more importantly, the higher your muscle and blood lactate levels can spike as a result of you exceeding your immediate aerobic engine ability (see the table on page 61).

You can quite easily start an aerobic base session with an anaerobic stress response if pace goes up too fast from 'resting' to upper Zone 1. That's not good if you want to be relaxed in the warm-up and enable your muscles to have coordinated movement patterns. This is the most common mistake of the time-crunched athlete. Don't rush your warm-ups and you have one of the secrets to achieving good aerobic fitness – for life.

Training energy output is very high compared to your usual daily activities, so ensure you take the time to warm up and plan how much energy you need for long sessions.

Energy expended in various activities

Mode	At Rest	Steady Training	Hard Training
Calories per hour	60-90	400–800	600–1,200 (>600% of rest)
Duration	24 hours	1–3 hours	0.5–1 hour
Repeatability	daily	daily	2–4 days per week
Limiting factor	ill health	patience	glycogen stores detraining
Total impact in calories	1,400–2,100	400–2,400	300–1,200

If you have ever had to start a commute ride fast because you're late, or have gone off with faster runners by mistake – you'll know that feeling:

You start heavy breathing quite quickly, the muscles feel heavy, and the stress is greater than you really wanted. It also takes ages to come back down – sometimes never in that session – only abating when you eventually stop exercising and start to cool down easily.

The commute, run session or over-zealous start to the swim session means it's too hard, too soon. Yet it was all in the warm-up execution. Being uncontrolled in your transition to the training session (and possibly choice of partners or course) was to blame. In the pool this happens if it's busy or if you self-seed wrongly in the lane and begin the first few lengths too fast. Soon you find yourself swimming in treacle, despite health and fitness being as good as normal. Efficient swimming was thrown out of the pool and you're fighting the water.

No one, whatever their fitness, can exclude a warm-up. It's not junk time; it's just never going to be at your race pace. That's why we call it warm-up and not race pace or intervals. Warm-ups must be below the

RIGHT NOW!

Look at all of your warm-up scenarios for swim, bike, run and strength-training sessions. Are you rushing? Trying to keep up? When you get it right, how does that session go? Make a list of warm-up habits that you must stick to. And stick to them, or you will be your own worst enemy.

average pace for a session. Even your top of Zone 1 is too stressful to start a session. Warm up properly and you will be feeling better and performing better physiologically.

How Long Should it Take?

The aerobic energy system takes time, whatever your level of fitness or ability, to kick several key chemical reactions into full effect. At a simple level – because that's all you need to know to justify starting slow – starting slow is good because it allows oxygen transport, lactate buffers, muscle temperature and neural firing to all, move from rest to exercise mode with less stress. It takes more than a couple of minutes for this to take full effect. This means you have to devote a few minutes to allowing the gradual transition to an acceptable training pace from your pre-training lifestyle activity.

If I could pick a magic number out of thin air (well, let's call it experience and research combined), I would say it takes at least ten (ideally, twenty) minutes or more, for the body's systems to be ready for moderate to hard exercise. If the warm-up is progressive and includes short bursts above your lactate threshold towards the middle or end of those 10–20 minutes, then it's enough to lead you into any time trial against the clock or race scenario.

So, the third rule of fit club means that you need to plan the early segments of your training (and racing) to take into account the time getting ready for the 'proper' training or racing against the clock. As much as Zone 1 training challenges people, I have seen those lacking in good aerobic fitness actually trying to race the warm-up to keep up with other more able people in a mixed ability group.

Take the time to warm up into sessions, especially those high quality turbo or track sessions. Like racing, you need time to warm up to prepare for quality training efforts.

'The First shall be Last'

It was a warm morning and the group session was about to begin. A mixed bunch, from very fast age-groupers to those learning about aerobic training, stood by the track. For many, track means effort, guts and glory. We were going to warm up on the grass inside the track. Warm-ups start with short-stride jogging, i.e. barely moving forward but still jiggling the bits we want to keep tight, and reminding the bowels what running can do for ... well ... being regular.

Straight away a few individuals shot away from the group – already striding. 'Easy!' came the call from the coach and the guilty parties briefly slowed down and shortened their strides. Again, they began to speed up. To counter this, the coach turned the group around so the fastest were now at the back and the slowest now dictated the pace at the front. The penny dropped for most of the guilty parties. With barely 300 yards covered, some runners (later to be seen as being well below the average running ability in the group) actually tried to lead the group, which included some quite handy runners.

The lesson was to start slow yet some had already wanted to rush ahead of their body's ability, to pretend they were faster than they actually were and to highlight that ability is never shown in the warm-up. It's in racing where true ability is measured and achieved.

Fourth Rule: Block Your Training

OK – so now you know you have goals and time to train, but the key most important thing that effective amateur and pro athletes do is quite simple: they plan building and recovery phases. Call it 'training' and 'adaptation' if you prefer. While there are many ways people have used training macro and micro cycles, I prefer to go back to the basic underlying physiological principle: that we are on a four-week cycle. This is clearly evident in the female menstrual cycle, which is around 28–9 days. OK, men may not have a clear physiological manifestation like women. However, men are humans, too (trust me on this) and live on the same planet. The need for a 3:1 mentality

Training weeks when you can back off and relax – even take time to enjoy social stuff instead of always doing goal-focused 'workouts' – are vital long-term for the tri-lifestyle.

to your training–recovery balance stems right back to your big annual goal event. Let me explain ....

If you work back every fourth week from your big goal race week, you can set in place an adaptation week in the training cycle. This week allows the body to recover hormonally from the training load, allows athletes to get used to easing off training rather than having 'just one more big week', and it allows admin and the rest of life to get some time of its own. In practice, you might find it hard to back off for a week, particularly when you feel that training is going well. But back off you must. It's the best way forward.

However, I think the adaptation week in a three-week training/one-week reduced training works so well because:

- **Over-training is so rife.** Ensuring seven out of twenty-eight days to still train but allow adaptation by easing off really does mean that training gets absorbed. Those athletes always trying to beat last week eventually hit the fatigue/injury/demotivation zone and have to ease off dramatically – ironically, often for *more* than seven days. If you plan the adaptation ahead of time, then you're more likely to train when it's the key focus of the week and enter the adaptation seven days happy that you're following a plan.
- **Most are not on plan.** Despite the reams of magazine, online and coach-initiated plans, few are actually on a plan – and if they are, these are most likely to be haphazard. I've come to this conclusion over years of quizzing athletes I know, for whom I have perhaps done bike-fitting or who ask questions about their training at shows and race exhibitions. *Some top level athletes do not always do what they've been asked to do.* Amazingly, when such athletes do prescribed training carefully planned by a team of experts, they improve more than those still racing the steady stuff or unable to do high intensity efforts because of fatigue. If nothing else, planning down-time makes you

hungry to train properly because you see the bigger point of training: to stress, then allow adaptation.

■ **It works!** Enough said.

From looking at published data on athletes and at most published research on endurance training, there are always adaptation periods. The line of training volume (or miles, if that's your currency of training) does not just go up and up and up a bit more. It is planned – even in short-term, high-intensity studies – to have a period of reduced training load *before* the effectiveness of that regime is put to the test or the athlete moves to the next phase of training. Few are this deliberate in their planning about future training – in fact, training usually starts with great gusto in October or November, and athletes will try to do the same thing all the time (except more of it) until the season arrives. Plan effectively, and you step back from the noise of the masses and think on a higher level – which achieves a higher performance level. Now, who wouldn't want that?

So, you've set out when you will be absorbing, rather than continuing, the training stress at its highest levels. Now you can plan more non-training activities to keep life, family and your work in better balance. *Kerching!*

The big challenge is to blend these adaptation weeks into what is often a less-than-perfect scenario. Here are a few examples and how to best make your 3:1 planning work:

> ## RIGHT NOW!
>
> Look at your big goal for this year, then work backwards every four weeks in your diary, heading it 'Adaptation Week'.

Adaptation week has an event in it. Yes, this often happens. A lesser event, perhaps an annual ritual or a favourite small local race, lands smack bang in the adaptation week. Fear not. You can still race, include intervals and be let out of cotton-wool – it's just that you should not throw every ounce of motivation and energy that you've built up in an adaptation week into a session or event that's small fry. You will need that energy and motivation for the forthcoming three weeks of training, so your efforts in an adaptation week must be measured. No more than is required and based on how you're feeling health and mojo-wise. Never, ever, ever do a tiny event or group hammer session if it's clear that you're ill, injured or incapable of motivating yourself 'up' for it. Your week must allow adaptation, so everything must be geared towards that aim. Simple.

I've planned a big week with my mates in the adaptation week. OK, so planning is not always all about you. If a big opportunity to train lands in your lap, you must move the weeks around. You still need to adapt, most importantly after this overload week. You must also go into a big week with normal health and ready to train – so allow for a slight reduction in training intensity leading up to the week and ensure that your muscle glycogen is on the high side by having a 2–3 day focus on high-carb, low-effort training. Tell your mates the same advice so you all get the chance to do this week's training well. If someone comes on a training camp, I always tell them that the three days leading up to the flight day must be next to zero training, eat well and clear the decks of work-tasks so you can focus on the job in hand.

I didn't get it all done in the third week of the training phase. Yes, there are those who think that every session must be done. I like honesty in an athlete's training diary, but I worry that athletes who do every session

they plan (or which their coach plans) must be ignoring their own body's signals concerning injury or fatigue. No one session is the key to being race-ready or getting fitter. You can miss a long run due to a sore foot, halve a long ride as you're forced inside due to the weather; even take three days off over the week because of unexpected work issues or family illness. It's not what missing a session does to your fitness, but what you *perceive* it does for your fitness that's most important.

For many, pool-time is the hardest to do when time crunched so you sometimes have to train on your own. Take a plan with you to get a full session done.

When Training just isn't Part of the Programme

At a training camp Scott Neyedli, Ironman winner and Scottish WTC Ironman record-holder (a speedy 8 hours 17 minutes), once told me that on one occasion he had got to the pool, entered the changing-room – even had everything with him to do the session. Yet he turned around and went home knowing that he was tired and needed the evening to relax, not train. Despite being on an Ironman training regime, he was more than able to drop a swim and not squeeze it elsewhere in the week. It was a planned session, never to be done. And this has happened more than once.

I feel worse in the adaptation week. Are you losing fitness and gaining weight by the week's end? OK, this reeks of exercise addiction, of a lack of understanding in how your body adapts and a complete ignorance of the feeling any athlete has at the end of a taper or adapting week. You *must* have recovery: your body is not an 'always-on' system like the internet or a factory machine. Intervals are better with recovery in between to create a precise change in body chemical status that ensures optimal training load – you don't stack four 8-minute intervals back to back; they need to have several minutes of very light recovery in between. Similarly, big weeks in effort or volume terms must eventually let up and allow adapting to this stimulus. No let up, no point in training.

Adapting to Adaptation Week

For me, adaptation weeks require more self-discipline than big training weeks. While my big training weeks are physically tough, my adaptation week is psychologically much more challenging. Like most athletes, I enjoy the feel-good factors and ego-boost you get when you complete a big training block or nail a key session. Having neglected recovery in the past, at first it was hard to get my head round the concept that you can get fitter while doing less!

Once I changed my mindset to focus on the bigger picture of doing well in my goal races, and be not filling out an impressive-looking training diary, then it all started to make sense! Sounds obvious, but it's amazing how easy it is to overlook this. During my adaptation week I find it useful to switch off from social media where everyone seems to be bragging about their latest training conquests! Now I find that I am able to put out better quality sessions during my hard weeks and actually embrace the down-time during my easy week. It also makes the taper into big races feel less of a shock to the system.

VICKY GILL, *Bronze medallist ETU long course triathlon 2014, Outlaw 2013 winner with 9 hour 42 minutes Ironman personal best*

Make training fun! Pick varied routes and enjoy being outdoors – that's a valuable gain that research studies on fitness fail to measure. You are not an engine; you need to smile regularly.

I've had a bad month, and the adaptation week is actually a week when I have time off, and I feel the need to train a lot. OK, again the areas of work, family and life events don't all work around your little training plan and the event you most want to do well in during the upcoming season. As long as you plan to have some adaptation soon after, it's OK – but do not turn this big week into the start of a four-week training block. It's your choice, but perhaps take a light week immediately after your time off 'training' week, and move the adaptation a week later. You must still train with a volume and intensity that is common sense – sadly the below 'happy' level of training you've had for the past month cannot be crammed into one week. Get up to training consistently, vary the load with longer/shorter days and don't forget to use some of that spare time to get brownie points in the bank.

Although it may seem as though I am talking 'pro' lifestyle to someone who is not a 'pro', bear with me. Try to get at least one or two naps in the day over your week off. This allows you to recharge in a week that's way above your normal training with a simple down-time of, say, forty-five minutes. Headphones on, long-haul face mask – or, my favourite, a 'mind machine' designed for sleeping – and you can recover like the best athletes on the planet. When sports scientists put elite African runners under the microscope recently by comparing them to European counterparts, the scientists found that the African runners had some physiological differences (e.g. smaller calves, living at altitude). Significantly, African runners sleep eleven hours a day rather than the nine hours slept by European runners. That is 22 per cent of a free commodity that helps recovery and is available to all who see it as vital to endurance sports excellence and achievement. Simple.

My work is really haphazard and planning up or down weeks is never actually going to work. OK, I get this scenario often and have devised a way to work with the athlete's lifestyle – that is, after all, what coaching is all about: personal solution delivery to help final performance outcomes. In this case, you still need to plan, but on a much more reactive basis that cannot be written four months ahead. It may be that four days ahead is your limit, so what's the solution?

Keep a diary to allow you to see what is and is not being done. In this way, your priorities for the next seven to ten days can still be laid out. You may have to do things that are higher in priority rather than train on a whim, but that is how the most effective athletes train. Many have a menu of sessions and do them when it fits with their upcoming week. Actually, in real life, very few can build work and life around their training plan.

No one actually follows a plan that is a perfect copy, exactly as it was written months in advance. Hence, it's as much an art as a 'clip and copy' action. Once this is taken into account, if you are just such

Training is great when you are fit and the plan falls into place nicely. Appreciate it – you've earned it.

an 'up in the air' person, the best way to tackle this is to learn that you are actually doing the right things to keep your sport and SWOT in balance – it's just that you never know what the next few weeks are going to bring

Yes, but I don't really get enough done on my training weeks to need that fourth week of 'recovery'. Really? Well, in this case you are not following a progressive plan. You are merely doing the same or repetitive sessions with training monotony high on the agenda. If you plan to have a recovery week it means, by deduction, that you have planned something significant to need recovery from. If you just enjoy training, then don't change; so long as you're happy, I am. You'll find plenty of other useful tips in this book, but perhaps training science is not your thing. Smile at the finish line, by all means, but do not expect to be at your best – ever.

I have several events and they don't all occur at four weeks apart so I don't know which one I should plan to work the 3:1 ratio around. Wow, this is planning at a level most try to ignore in a vain attempt to do it all and race their best every time. I would suggest there needs to be one primary event that is hardest or the one you most want to do well at. Let's be honest – no one actually thinks every race is the same: we all have favourite distances, types of course or particular people to beat. You still need tapers to these other important events, but your primary goal takes the lead. The longer the races, the greater your need to recover. Conversely, short events can be done back to back. Even this short racing scenario needs some recovery weeks (your adaptation time), though they may not be perfectly four weeks apart.

Just as long as some adapting and recovery from racing is taken into account some athletes manage to always be slightly out on their four-weekly cycle. If you take adaptation as part of your training, then you have already become wise to the obsessive 'more-is-better' mentality that can take hold when people get fitter, get racing or get beaten.

Listen to your body and feed it when more fuel is needed or rest it when fatigue is higher than it should be. Be balanced; don't react single-mindedly.

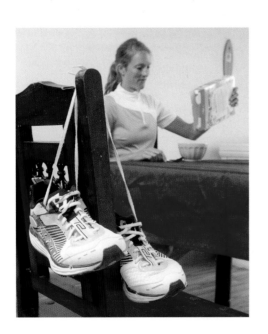

A Hit to the Ego

'When I first contacted you I already had in mind of how I should go about constructing a new and improved training schedule of twenty hours per week.

I believed that this increased training volume would improve me enough to be competitive for my target race, which was the World Sprint-Distance Triathlon Championships being held in London during September 2013.

Being an avid listener to your podcast, I'd had some understanding that building a solid training base was imperative and that not introducing high intensity too early or too often was key. Also, that each session should have a goal or focus, whether it be recovery or strength, endurance etc. – basically not just working out without knowing why you had done so.

I'd expected your response to be how I might lay out my week and how to mix sessions, or when it's best to introduce some high-intensity sessions. I'd had hinted that cycling was my focus as I'd felt it was a weakness and needed improvement.

The actual advice I received was of greater value and made me reflect on my ideology behind training. You pointed out that twenty hours was a huge investment of time to set aside each week for a sprint distance event; that I had to be careful of fatigue burn-out; plus, would my home life be balanced?

It's funny thinking back as it was a hit to the ego. My wife also listened to your response and said that she agreed with you by pointing out more is not always the best policy; and my wife reminded me that I'd had fatigue issues in the past due to training in the red zone too often and racing way too much.

I'd only started triathlon in 2010.

I still wanted to up my hours per week, but 20 hours was no longer the magic number I felt was a 'must-do' to improve me enough to be competitive ....

I now realized I had to maximize my time so the impact of a higher training volume would be reduced on my young family; also, to structure a training plan which would have more realistic chance of being consistent. In one podcast you mentioned stealth training [getting training done using time wisely, such as running to work, i.e. 'commutes'], and this would now turn out to be my main way of training during the week as it was easier to be consistent and time-efficient.

Mid-week I ran to and from work and cycled on my lunch hour as I decided to set up a turbo trainer in the bike cage. I also set up a turbo trainer in our garden at home. I also timed sessions at the weekend to coincide with my daughter's morning sleeps and in the evening once she went to bed so that I was always around as per normal. By using the turbo trainer at home for 99.9 per cent of my bike session I was always available to my wife if she needed me or just wanted to pop out and talk, etc, while I trained.

By planning bike sessions around my wife's social schedule or even TV habits, she could see that I was trying to be considerate and that disappearing into the garden for 45 minutes to work out wasn't the end of the world.

Basically, all of the above points work towards the same end result: reducing stress and maximizing consistency (training smart), therefore increasing the fun factor, which I believe is the main reason for sport in the first place.'

CARL FANNON *(Australia), Dad, JBST iTunes podcast listener and Sprint Triathlon World Champion 35–39, London 2013*

CHAPTER FOUR

The Most Important Skill of All

Repeat this over and over – skill is the most important skill.

The very good athletes look very efficient. Their muscles do what is required with little excess movement – which means that more is going into getting to the finish line fast and less is wasted with unnecessary muscle use. Few athletes are ever absolutely perfect. Even they know they have slight technical imperfections. But they are very close to perfect. Very, very close. Think Michael Phelps, Laura Trott or David Rudisha.

Professionals have trained to be perfect and they never stop trying to improve their 'form'. The bottom line is that a person's oxygen-carrying ability, their VO_2max, can be used in better or worse ways during endurance sport by two other less thought about elements: cruise pace and economy of effort.

Cruise pace and economy of effort are two very trainable factors but, unlike VO_2max, you need to do things with precision to have the desired effect. Don't just head out the front door and start swimming, biking or running.

So, let's assume you train in Zone 1 and thus get a lot of your VO_2max oxygen-carrying efficiency done and dusted. That's the easy bit to get right. Most importantly, you must be thinking good stroke mechanics, correct bike ergonomics and running with good form in these sessions if you're to become skilled. Practice makes permanent (read that again, please!).

It is better to be more conscious of your best 'form' when training than always trying to catch up or stay ahead of another person. If you're not wearing a competitor's bib with a number on it or if you're taking part in a fun group session, please chill, enjoy this and think about *your* 'form', not someone else's idiotic ego speed-merchant's actions.

Cruise Faster

I define your cruise pace as 'the best pace you as an athlete can move while your muscles maintain an economical movement pattern'. *Note:* it is not a set pace; it varies depending on the sport, time of year and eventual goal distance of racing you wish to do. It may be mid to upper Zone 1 or low to mid Zone 2. This depends on:

1 Whether enough base training has been done to keep lactate levels low.
2 How relaxed the athlete can remain as pace increases.
3 Genetically endowed muscle and limb efficiencies.

The above three factors explain why elites train 20–35 hours to be very good at keeping lactate low. If lactate and other metabolites build up, they start to chemically affect the efficiency of muscle from within. Hence, at a critical level the form of all athletes will plummet. Low lactate training in Zone 1 ensures relaxed muscle contractions are pre-programmed to look super smooth. The fact that the athlete is able to think about what he or she is doing comes down to the following key factors:

It feels great to go fast, while in control and using all your muscles. However, it takes practice to keep below the point where you start to fight yourself.

■ Not being stressed chemically inside the muscle – let's call this 'no pain'.
■ Being able to monitor muscle movement because brain–oxygen delivery is good – let's call this 'clear brain'.

Professionals can listen to their body at a high level of detail and fine-tune it minutely in 'real time'. They constantly seek to perfect an already brilliant motor-programme in the nervous system to produce what we mortals see as perfection. Lots of practice makes a close to permanent perfect muscle action. For you to do this right, remember: 'No pain – clear brain'.

Top-End Technique

Although we know that Zone 1 training predominates in elite performers and that some of this is clearly focused on technique and some on race pace, 'tempo' in Zone 2 or high-end HIIT (see below) efforts in Zone 3 really do make muscle economy a few per cent better still. Though a raft of evidence shows very little of Zone 2 is actually performed by top triathletes, it does help to lock on race-pace feel, or to practise something at race pace such as feeding nutrition or bike handling. For example, if sipping a gel or downing a sports drink causes a slight increase in breathing rate and lactate, this can suddenly slow you from your normal race pace. You are untrained at this so are inefficient at it.

Thirty years ago marathoners shunned water in races and often in training, believing it would make them slower. Now age-group runners can be speeded up by ten minutes in a marathon by using smart nutrition. Interestingly, elite runners now have specific sessions that aim to take 15 g of carbohydrate every fifteen minutes (see www.bit.ly/TCTmara1 and www. bit.ly/TCTmara2).

If elites can run–cruise at sub-5-minute mile while running and drinking, the benefits to speed maintenance and muscle efficiency are very evident. At an amateur level, runners (and thus triathletes) who want to go longer distances have to practise feeding in training to get it more right than wrong as a 'skill' in events. I guess that it's the age-old adage: practise what you want to do on race-day so that it's no surprise to your muscles. Or brain. Or both.

Practise feeding on the bike, especially if you are a mid- and long-course triathlete. Feeding on the bike is a key part of your in-race skill set. Can you stay aerobic and feed on the go?

High-intensity Interval Training (HIIT)

Zone 3 hard intervals, often called HIIT, have been shown to improve economy, albeit by a small amount – but small amounts here beat no further gain in VO_2max elsewhere. Such improvements are simply the icing on the cake. But be warned: HIIT is not a short-cut for the weak-willed, for the time-crunched or impatient who think Zone 1 is 'junk' and too inferior to their big plans.

I am somewhat surprised that we still have articles, even books and plenty of evangelists, shouting about a new interval regime to help those with little time to train (minimal hours invested). That's rubbish. Think about it. If elites could train 1–2 hours and take 22–3 hours off, don't you think they would be doing just that? For your aerobic efficiency, fitness and skill level you have to put the time into the training bank – no short-cuts. So, be efficient with your time, but don't try to cram an eight-hour training week into two or three hours of spare time.

The elites who we hear about in performance terms are also the ones who have just the right muscle attachments, joint stability and nurture over the years before we hear about them. Many with talent and plenty of hard effort done early in their athletic career fail to continue to be good because their body breaks down. We never hear about them; they are collateral damage from the system of building champions way before that. When one potential champion is broken, another pushes his or her way to prominence. However, as you're the only version of you, let's be careful not to break you. I prefer to nurture people like you into athletes rather than nuke people like you while I search for champions.

You can't change your muscle, bone or injury history. Some age-groupers have rugby injuries, over-use on their run muscles, suffer serious accident joint surgery or have less than perfect muscle make-up for endurance sport. Hey, this is a broad church – you're all invited! It's just that these factors do limit your performance and must be taken into account when designing your sessions and training-plan tweaks. You're not Jamie Summers or Steve Austin – if the training plan breaks you, we cannot rebuild you and make you bionic.

I hope that by now you will have realized there are some missed weaknesses in your SWOT and you must own up to these now – doing so could save the whole project of 'Better You' in the long run. It's always easy to have training in mind but it's often more of a challenge to solve the conundrum: 'How do I use my time better to make more sessions happen correctly?' As the saying goes: you can't see it happening until you can 'see it' happening.

Cruise Pace and Race Ability

Here are some observations that have come from a variety of triathletes and which appear to help cruise pace and race ability:

1 Many triathletes have commented to me about feelings of effortless movement after a sports massage, Bowen Therapy session or similar personal favourite type of 'body work'. This may not be immediately apparent after the session; perhaps requiring an overnight sleep to have its affect felt. It's not an active 'training' session but it can help you to be efficient, keep track of muscle tightness and encourage you to get second opinions on how your body is faring.

2 The days when it just clicks and you never saw it coming are a result of all the previous days you were thinking about good technique. Good 'form' is not anyone's property – it must be earned by being cognizant of movement during all three sports. I would argue this includes transitions and things that you must be efficient at so as to save time and energy in your triathlon races. These include: getting ready to race (e.g. putting on your wetsuit), dealing with bike issues (e.g. changing bottles) and race idiosyncrasies (e.g. technical sections of the bike leg).

Quick Tip

Book yourself for regular body-work sessions. See such sessions as a vital part of training, not an afterthought or something to be done instead of training.

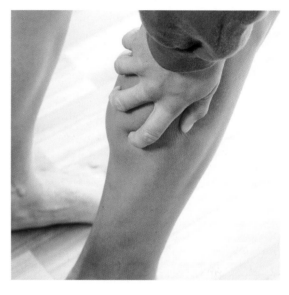

Invariably, you'll get issues with muscles as a result of training and racing. Don't try to battle through injuries; instead, use tried-and-tested body solutions to keep you uninjured.

Quick Tip

Always be thinking about good form as well as the demands of your races. You will always need to be planning some new skills to keep improving.

Quick Tip

Plan bigger volume/higher frequency of training weeks by having a focus on one sport for seven days, with minimal time put to the other two. This is a simple way to overload.

Quick Tip

Increase your chances of racing in the 'flow' by approaching each race with a clear mind. Focus on the job in hand – right here, right now – and not on the person in front of you or those chores you left at home. Great form in races comes from a mind clear of any other details.

Quick Tip

Jump into races with vigour and a child-like enthusiasm to learn. Don't see them as potentially ego-damaging, a chore or below your level of ability. Each athlete learns big lessons in every race.

3   The fluid swimming, biking and running that people observe several days into a training camp is no freak accident. Often athletes say to me that they are a bit tired when starting the sessions, but they feel efficient (and if eating and drinking enough) with a more 'natural' movement pattern. The increased frequency and volume of training just makes movement better, up to a point. After a certain number of hours people get tired, make silly mistakes and should rest rather than train. They have surpassed their 'sweet spot' of training volume.

4   Races where you can go as fast as you like seem to occur when you were chilled and felt fit. This combination of relaxed, fit muscles and a mindset clear of self-doubt and other people's race performance really do help you race in the moment (or in the 'flow'). It may happen once or twice a season. For some, over certain distances it happens just once. It *never* happens by forcing it.

5   Doing the practical beats reading about it. You have to do it to know what the task of triathlon actually demands of you. I could explain in detail every aspect of triathlon, but practical application is vital. By all means use *Time-Crunched Triathlon* to point you in the right direction. However, you don't want to over-analyse, confuse and lose track of the real-world nature of triathlon. It's not an equation but an

experience. Practise racing to be a racing practitioner because until you can see yourself doing it you're merely a theoretical triathlete.

6 Trying to keep up with another athlete as your number one game plan from the 'off' does not help a training session or race. Other athletes may have weaker, stronger, slower or faster sections – and you'll just end up shadowing them. How will that help you? Unless you're racing the new draft-legal sprint triathlon format where drafting on swim and bike are sensible (though not the only game plan), most amateur athletes have splits that vary considerably, yet final times can be very similar. To be fluid you must concentrate on your pacing, your body's signals and perhaps go with your instinct to push where your rival could be weaker or hesitant. To get the best from you, you must focus on you.

Although others can help to push you hard in quality sessions, the scope of most training is controlled (i.e. skilful), aerobic practice (CAP).

> ## Quick Tip
>
> Before each training session and race, clear your mind of what others are doing and think just about what *you* are going to focus upon. Being mindful beats being a sheep.

Training is not time to day-dream or think about work. Instead, be in the moment, focus on your best form and learn what an 'efficient you' feels like.

Being aware that bike-to-run is a skill you practise regularly is to be aware that you are not a biker or a runner, but a 'bike-to-runner' triathlete.

Skill is Never off Your Mind

I don't know what your particular best triathlon time-crunched sessions are. However, Chapter 5 is full of effective sessions you can follow and with its tips, can provide suggestions to hone in on your performances or weaknesses and point you towards some of your best returns on training invested. Central snorkel swimming, indoor cycle rollers, treadmill micro intervals or putting on run shoes with elastic laces. Any or all of them could just be fun or they could be a greatest leap in skill you have had for months, even years.

When fitness across all three sports reaches your maximum level – very hard to achieve simultaneously for most of us – it doesn't just stay there. Many factors such as ageing, injuries, poor dietary balance, ill-health and accidents can knock it backwards. However, despite not being at your fittest, you can still practise good form, keep efficiency as a real-time goal and therefore advance in your quest to be a master of three entirely different trades.

Elite athletes in single sports may rarely venture into other sports. Cyclists need not swim. Swimmers need not run or cycle. Runners may not be able to ride a bike. The very fact that you're trying to do all three means you're challenging conventional single-sport training wisdom, ideas and methods.

Use your **SWOT Analysis** form in Appendix 2 (see pages 211–5). You should always be looking at what you do in training, and ensure that skill work happens every week and is informed by your race experiences and training hindsight. Skill should never be off your mind.

I Sat Down in Transition and Read Another Chapter of My Book

My first tri experience shows the importance of practising. The first triathlon I entered was the London Olympic distance. I had a new bike and went out a couple of times a week and managed to run a few times a week as well, but with no real structure. My swimming really took a back seat if anything else came along. I didn't have a wetsuit and I'd never swum in open water before.

Before I knew it, the race was a week away and I had to hire a wetsuit. Lucy, my girlfriend, didn't pick it up until the night before. I'd read you should practise getting out of a wetsuit to speed up your transition time, so my one and only practice was me standing under the shower for a minute, then running into the lounge dripping wet and pulling my wetsuit off! It wasn't too hard so I didn't think it was a big deal!

The next day I got to the race early and chilled out reading my book lying in transition. I looked the part I think – but looks can be deceptive!

When my wave was called into the water I had no idea just how deceptive looks can be. Literally, after about ten strokes I couldn't turn my arms over, I couldn't breathe and I seriously thought I was done for. I toughed it out though with the aid of breaststroke, and staggered up the ramp out of the water smiling (with relief, I think).

I then started walking towards transition, chatting to a big guy about how hard that had been. Then, led by my girlfriend, all the nearby spectators yelled at me to get running. It took me a further seven minutes to get out on my bike – which I actually fell off mounting as I hadn't practised much with my cleats!!!

To this day, Lucy says I sat down in transition and read another chapter of my book!

JASON SWINDON, *film studio carpenter and Ironman 70.3 finisher*

CHAPTER FIVE

Ten Effective Training Sessions

In this chapter I'll be sharing with you ten of my tried and tested training sessions that you'll find really effective. These sessions all have plenty of scope for you to personalize them to make them even more effective for you. Note that they are not the only ten sessions you will ever need to know (be very wary if someone tells you that fib). However, each has a history that means that the principle behind it, the tips to get the best out of it, and (most importantly) ways to alter it for variety, are already refined. Alter each session as and when required, and don't stop thinking differently. Having said that, don't change a session just for the hell of it; you must have a rock-solid reason for doing so. Just trying to be different doesn't make training more effective.

I like the idea of assessing athletes to get concrete data. Weight, maximum heart rate, accurate time trial ability – they all give an honesty that appeals. On the other hand, short courses, rough guesses or outright lies never help you to perfect your training and race technique; they just give your ego a false polish. Avoid that with better, more effective training sessions.

RIGHT NOW!

Look at your training diary and see what sessions really appear to work for you. Are any of them in my top ten below? You may be doing a session that I've not yet thought about. If a session appears not to be working for you, don't hesitate – drop it and try one of the other sessions in this chapter. Your training must evolve by throwing out the obsolete and harnessing any fitter, smarter sessions you come across.

Here is my top ten list of effective training sessions:

1 Swim assessment
2 Swim stamina blocks
3 Swim open water
4 Bike strength–endurance
5 Rollers
6 Tri position acclimation or perfection
7 Brick run
8 Run adversity
9 Hill economy efforts
10 Time trial tests

It is notoriously difficult to obtain real data for swim courses, but a pool is a measurable and exact distance, and can allow for easy video analysis/ feedback.

Ideally, seek the help of your personal coach, club coach, or a friend with superior swim ability and knowledge. To get the numbers is important, but it's best practice to capture the swim on video so your session can be analysed properly afterwards, with helpful feedback on what needs to be focused upon. *Note:* If other members of the public are around, there may be restrictions on filming so check with your pool supervisor first.

SESSION 1: Swim Assessment

Equipment
one other person
video camera
stopwatch
swim stroke feedback form (see
Appendix 2 on pages 218–19)
pen/pencil

Quick Tip

Pick a less busy time to complete this, so you're not aided by drafting or hindered by others just out for a leisurely swim.

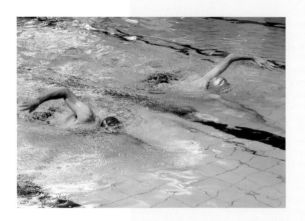

You may warm up and swim the assessment with others, but be sure to keep on plan for the session to obtain reliable and accurate data.

Performance Benefits

If you know how to pace a time trial and what the expected race speed is, then you're more likely to be able to swim more consistent swim-splits. You'll also get a better feel for swim-speed versus perceived effort in sessions. If you don't actually know what time you've just swum for that steady set of 200 metres, how can you rate your efficiency, recovery and fitness?

Never think it's good just because you've kept up with the feet in front – that's drafting their pace, not swimming yours. To be able to predict how you will perform in a pool, and therefore very roughly what you can do in open water, is not a good party trick – it's a vital swim skill. Repeat: *vital* swim skill.

Prior Mindset and Focus

Be ready to vary effort as required and to give it full gas in the time trial. No excuses! This is how good you are at swimming. Be ready to remember numbers and jot them down on a notepad soon after on the poolside.

Warm-Up

■ 5–8 × 100 metres relaxed with 20 seconds recovery (known as 20" RI) between.

■ Do this relaxed and focus on gradually warming up and catching water properly.

Swimming is very cerebral; you should be relaxed and focusing on good technique across all four limbs – simultaneously.

Main Session

- Stroke sets 3 × 200 metres (taking the least number of strokes possible).
- Aim for good clean push-offs, smooth swimming and consistent stroke counts on the fourth and eighth length.
- It may not be race relevant or anything other than minimal effort swimming, but it does prove that you can be smooth through the water.
- 3 × 50 metres with 60 second recovery (60" RI) sculling in between.
- Approximate push-off distance, total stroke-count and finishing heart-rate (count for 6 seconds and add a zero).

Power Set

- 4 × 25 metres maximal sprint effort with a minimum of 120" RI.
- Time your effort exactly. Attempt to set a personal best every rep!
- Follow with a very easy 100 metres of mixed swimming; there is no rush here to move quickly to the next set. Here comes the key benchmark, so only start it when fully ready.

Time Trial

- 400 metres of best-effort swim – aim to swim as fast as your current fitness allows, but do not blow up by swimming unrealistically (video footage is really useful when/if the stroke falls apart).
- Time the effort exactly – noting 200-metre split.

Stroke Set

- After recovery from 400-metre time trial, 1 × 200 – least strokes possible at a relaxed (Zone 1) speed.
- Note stroke count on fourth and eighth lengths.

Cool-Down

- 300 metres of 'perfect tempo stroke' broken into 50 seconds.
- Remind your muscles of good stroke mechanics at a mid-range speed.
- Focus on good body position in the water and relaxed breathing.

Post-Session

- Quick carbohydrate recovery snack.
- Discuss any major stroke weaknesses with your coach/observer.
- Write down stroke pointers and lessons learned.

Ways to Advance or Customize

The time trial may be increased to test for speed–endurance, but 400 metres gives a good pace judgement and swim-ability benchmark. Repeating the process every 1–2 months in season, or occasionally off-season, is a handy reminder of exactly where you are swim-wise.

You could also try the 400-metre time trial in a wetsuit, but perhaps earlier in the session to help reduce the effects of heat build-up in an indoor pool. For expert swim input, see www.swimfortri.com.

If Zone 1 steady-state, aerobic and/or technique-focused swimming is the majority of training to be a competitive swimmer, then good old-fashioned bread-and-butter stamina swims are a mainstay of your swim diet. Such sessions will help you to develop time in the water to 'feel' the various postural, propulsive and breathing aspects of a well-honed stroke. No single drill, interval effort regime or land-based activity cuts through this necessary aerobic swim base. Triathlons are 10 per cent aquatic and 90 per cent on land, so it's worth keeping in balance speed gains and return on time invested in trying to be a swim perfectionist. For many, a well-planned tri club swim or masters session will fit the bill – sometimes. However, you may need to be self-contained with some swim stamina work. Also, such sessions need not always be an hour long, so lunchtime 30–40 minute swims will suffice – ideal for time-crunched you! See Session 2 on page 87.

SESSION 2: Swim Stamina Blocks

Equipment
A pool with some lane etiquette in place.

Performance Benefits
This gives you good aerobic training of the upper body (vital as few people are naturally aerobic with their arms). If you're focusing on good technique, with repeatable swim-sets that combine to give 1, 2, 3k or more, then you're doing the aquatic equivalent of 'time in saddle' or 'steady run miles'. You create less lactate so you can increase pace subtly and swim for longer without undue fatigue. Pools may only be 25 metres – well, 50 metres, if you're lucky to swim 'long course' – so you have to build length after length after length. Thousands of lengths combine to hone your swimming, but you must always be aware of your technique. Aerobic swim muscles are great race-day performers.

Prior Mindset and Focus
Be relaxed and realistic about how much of this session or a similar type of endurance you can get done. Don't try to get too many metres into say 40 minutes, such that you swim the whole thing at 'tempo' with little chance to relax. It's Zone 1 time, so relax.

Warm-Up
- Start with 6 × 50 metres as 25 metres front crawl, then your own choice of another stroke back.
- Swim 4 × 100 metres relaxed, with 20 seconds recovery interval (RI).
- Focus on gradually increasing effort in the 100 seconds to feel fully aerobically ready by this stage.

Main Session
- 8–10 × 100 metres of bilateral front crawl: 75 per cent effort; 30 seconds recovery or 30" RI.

- 8–12 × 25 metres of bilateral front crawl: 80 per cent effort; 20" RI.
- 4–6 × 100 metres of bilateral front crawl: 75 per cent effort; 30" RI.
- Simple no-nonsense aerobic swim-blocks, with repeats ideally staying similar across the sets.

Cool-Down

- 200–300 metres of 'perfect tempo stroke' broken into 50-metre blocks.
- I like the idea of going a little bit over your longer distance swim-speed capability at the end as this allows you to feel how much your muscles are fatigued or not. Too easy and you always feel good.

Post-Session

No drama: it's just a bread-and-butter session. Note the approximate times for each set and have a recovery snack within the hour. Otherwise get on with your day; there's nothing to see here.

Ways to Advance or Customize

You're a multi-sport athlete so you can make these sessions more applicable to triathlon by adding a running element. Not outside the pool in your cossie, but deep-water running (DWR) with a flotation belt such as the Speedo Hydro belt. This way you get a low-impact aerobic run time, which has been shown to be as good as running on terra firma. It's also just a click on and off transition so you lose no training time, but do get to mix swim and run training. It's ideal in the winter when run conditions are not so good, or when muscles are sore from a hard race or reeling from a run interval session. Also, it keeps you in the pool for longer, gives you better value for money, and adds run training into what would otherwise be just a swim day. Consequently, it's perfect multi-sport endurance dovetailing.

If you're a pool-based triathlete the principles are still the same: use your race kit to see how it functions and feels. For open water some of your testing and practice can take place in (ideally) a long-course (50 metres), an indoor pool or even an outdoor lido. Using a 'speedsuit' (search 'Open water full suits' on Google) or a thin-skin wetsuit indoors makes swimming faster, so you get to feel, practise and extend the range of speeds you can swim at. Also, assume one stroke to one metre. As you may be swimming in a pool of an old-fashioned or random length, whether in open water or a pool, use the 100 metres to denote 100 strokes when you don't know the exact measurement (e.g. if in open-water lake).

However, cold water acclimatization, sighting above water and dealing with choppy conditions have to be prioritized once you enter the last 4–12 weeks before the race season. Getting to a weekly open water (O/W) swim is ideal preparation for the real world of swimming with no black line to follow or lane ropes to smooth the water. Always keep warm before and after the swim – see www.dryrobe.com.

SESSION 3: Swim Open Water

Equipment
race wetsuit
normal tri clothing
swim cap
old run shoes/sandals
warm-up pull cords

Performance Benefits
Saving energy by swimming in a straight line between buoys, knowing how long it will take you to put on the wetsuit properly – and I mean *properly* – all takes practice. I know of athletes who have trained 10–20 hours for triathlon, then arrived at the swim start late, not got their suit on properly, missed the start-off, and very nearly bottled it because of the stress they found themselves under. The more relaxed you are in a wetsuit, the better you will swim in real triathlon scenarios.

Quick Tip

I would also suggest using a swim safety float (e.g. ChillSwim tow donut or similar), which you can attach to your waist. The device floats above the water, making you much more visible, and gives you a safe place in which to store keys, a GPS unit or run shoes.

Prior Mindset and Focus

Give yourself time, be sure to have safety cover in place (and a tow device for added visibility), and relax. If in open water, always wait for others so you have safety in numbers. In a lido, look for the best lane to seed yourself, then relax. This session is not made better by being stressed.

Warm-Up

Use this session to perfect a dry land warm-up with low-resistance swim cords (sometimes called bungees) and land-based resistance 'cordz'. This allows you to perfect the right resistance level and duration of warm-up for race-day and be ready to swim soon after immersion into the water.

- 100 metres as front crawl; relaxed stroke, not rushing the press phase – take 20" RI sculling.
- 100 metres as 25 metres with head up sighting forwards, 25 metres as front crawl – 20" RI sculling.
- 100 metres as 25 metres catch-up (focus on press-phase), 25 metres front crawl – 20" RI sculling.
- 200 metres as straight swim but accelerate for 10 strokes five times in the course of the 200 metres.

Main Session

You're now ready for some faster swimming, so get your head in gear – it's the high-intensity lactate set coming next.

Lactate Set

100 metres swum all out – if in the pool, note time; if unable to note time, assess based on acceleration, holding speed and final lactate sensation (all things should point to it being hard).

Getting into a wetsuit can be time-consuming. It's not like pulling on a T-shirt or a pair of shorts. Take time to do it well, but allow this time before every race or you will be stressed and waste energy.

Then, with no rest, do 400 metres at 80 per cent fast-cruise effort – for the first part of the swim you will be breathing very hard, using both sides to breathe and wondering if you can get your breath back. (You do – it just takes time so relax, breathe plenty and wait for the lactate build-up and oxygen deficit to disappear.)

Now chill for a few minutes.

Speed Set

- Swim 6–8 × 50 metres front crawl as 25 metres maximum pace then 25 metres cruise pace.
- Have at least 1 minute 30 seconds light sculling, floating or standing (but *not* hanging off a lane rope or buoy). This clears lactate and allow breathing and muscle function to return to normal.

Tolerance Set

- Swim 3–5 × 175 metres as the first 75 metres flat-out, then hold on at 80 per cent for the next 100 metres.
- Allow a full three minutes for correct recovery after each one.

Cool-Down

4 × 50 metres very easy, relaxed stroke at moderate effort, feeling strong in the water and concentrating on the first parts of your stroke that you know will fall away as fatigue hits home.

Post-Session

Hard efforts mixed with the possibility of cold water mean a small snack and dressing up warm are essential. Upper and lower body compression wear would be ideal. If you do follow this with a bike session, be sure to have options warmer than normal on hand as you will be losing heat and must not get cold for the sake of it.

Ways to Advance or Customize

Rather than making this session ever bigger, look at increasing the speed or distance travelled per hard effort. Maybe even notice that you can control breathing faster after efforts. It's about quality improving, not more and more reps. It can be fun to turn some of the efforts into group races over a set distance in the pool or to buoys in open water. Racing with others around you is the name of the game in tri.

SIMPLE TIME MANAGEMENT FROM THE BOSS

'If you can manage your time well, try to organize training to be around or with other people so it makes the training seem easier. Even if an organized masters swim, club run, or club cycle is less than you planned, it's always nice to have company before you make up the extra time or miles on your own.

If practical, use running or cycling to get to work – this gives you some extra miles for free. To optimize the morning commute, do this fasted (no breakfast beforehand). It will help turn the session into a fat-burning exercise, helping to lose fat weight a little easier.

If you're an early bird, choosing a pool for a pre-work session close to your place of work can save time in traffic from your normal routine. [*Note:* Scott is *not* an early bird!]

Although my work isn't flexible with lunch breaks, many companies are. This can be a good time to head out for a steady tempo run, small swim session, gym/core workout or treadmill-spin session.

If you're a gym monkey and enjoy spin classes I suggest you complete the class, then hit the treadmill soon afterwards to help simulate a brick workout simulating T2 in races.

A cycle turbo class with a tri- or cycle club can be the starting point for a brick session. If you don't have access to a lot of treadmills, then simply all have your run shoes handy and nip out for a 10–20 minute run loop.'

Scott Neyedli, *Ironman winner (twice), Scottish WTC Ironman Record Holder (8 hours 17 minutes) and full-time worker*

This next session will help with your bike strength–endurance.

SESSION 4: Bike Strength–Endurance

Equipment

Indoors:	*Outdoors:*
turbo trainer	race bike
race bike	helmet
electric fan	spares
towel	tri cycle shoes
sports drink	sports drink (e.g. 50 grams
bike shorts	PowerBar IsoActive in
base layer shirt	750 millilitres of water)
heart rate belt/watch	bike shorts
	cycle shirt
	base layer
	heart rate belt/watch

Performance Benefits

Endurance riding teaches your muscles to be coordinated in circles and there's no short-cut to making your muscles efficient – you've got to get the miles in. However, for many, indoor riding is time-efficient in start-up, reduces start-stop riding in traffic, and can help if local weather/light conditions/terrain are not conducive to safe and effective riding intensity. By using phases of over-geared riding, defined as riding at around 50–60 revs per minute 'cadence' around threshold power (certainly above Olympic distance tri power or effort), you get to strengthen your muscles specifically in race position. For further details, see this video: http://bit.ly/1yYedg8.

Low cadence work results in a lower HR despite quite high power output. Though you may not have power measurement, you're looking to be using bigger gears to drop cadence and result in an effort level (perceived at the legs, not the lungs) as moderate to hard.

Prior Mindset and Focus

This need not be a long session but the effort when pushing the over geared efforts (OGE) means that you're working the legs like a strength session. If you really are not ready to push, then turn the session into a purely aerobic endurance session, and keep the cadence modest (85–95 revs per minute) with a Zone 1 heart rate focus. Many people split their longest ride and OGE into separate days, with some doing both on the same session, but this mixture of say 2–3 hours with OGE included is a hard work-out and you have to be ready for such overload.

Pushing the pedals down with force while relaxing your upward-moving leg is the simple key to riding well. It is definitely not a case of trying to push or pull around the entire circle of a pedal revolution.

Warm-Up

- Ride in an easy to moderate gear for the first 15–20 minutes at around 75–85 rpm, moving through low to mid-Zone 1. Don't be in a rush.
- Drink 100–200 millilitres of energy drink at this point (and about every 15 minutes thereafter) to prime your brain for the moderately hard work – if you bonk, your bike quality wanes and you will recover much more slowly.

Main Session

- Start with 3 × 5–6 minutes seated at 55–60 revs per minute (if outdoors, choose a consistent climb; if indoors, set resistance moderate to high)
- Heart rate will build gradually from about 75 per cent to 83 per cent of HRmax. It will feel hard on the legs but HR will look strangely lower than you would expect.
- Use approximately 1–4 minutes spinning at 90 rpm between efforts.
- If you have power measurement on your turbo trainer, gym bike or race bike, this can keep your efforts more precise. Typically,

the OGE effort is around 75 per cent of your maximum power from a ramp test (around FTP or 'threshold' power) and recoveries at 40 per cent of max power or light Zone 1 riding.

Cool-Down

- Riding back home (or for 10–20 minutes if indoors in a light gear) allows your legs to relax and for recovery to start.
- If you're looking to maximize recovery, it's time to sip a quality protein recovery shake.
- You may add an easy 'shake out' run of 10 minutes, but don't be tempted to turn this into an epic bike-run every time.

Post-Session

- Muscles have been pushed at a high load so go easy for the next 12–24 hours.
- Quality carbs and protein foods are the building blocks and recovery fuels to ensure you get the strength adaptation underway and muscles are ready to train in a day or so.
- Do two of these sessions back to back *and* fuel incorrectly, and you will hit a BIG fatigue wall.

Ways to Advance or Customize

- This can be increased to 4–5 × 8–10 minutes, though the key is not to do the effort at ever higher wattages but to extend the duration or slightly lower the cadence.
- Do not go below 50 rpm, and be sure you keep this overload effort away from key race-days or time trial efforts.

Though three-drum contraptions make many triathletes sweat with fear, they are a superb way to get more efficient and to learn to balance the bike, thus helping you to save energy when you're riding in real-world conditions. It takes time to move from wearing run shoes and holding the wall the whole time to being able to clip-in, ride, take your hands off, and do your song selection on your mp3 player.

SESSION 5: Rollers

Equipment

one set of rollers
cycle shorts
cycle top
electric fan (*optional*)

bottle with a low-calorie sports
drink (*optional*)
Beginners: old run shoes
Experts on rollers: cycle shoes

Performance Benefits

Riding on rollers is akin to riding on ice. It teaches you to pedal smoothly, to use the hips to control the bike, and to relax the upper body. A rotating wheel has a fair amount of gyroscopic force once you get up enough speed: so the wheels, once moving sufficiently, actually balance you – however you need to balance in-sync with the wheels. I have seen clients begrudgingly agree to get rollers blossom into someone who can ride them for an hour and be engaged in riding, enjoy the time, and not get bored as they would on a turbo trainer. Rollers engage you, so you become better engaged with your bike. I also believe their simplicity of set up helps them to be useful for run warm-ups and varied skill brick sessions – even race cool-downs.

Rollers are not for everyone but they really can help to make you a smooth pedaller. Use them to practise to improve your pedal action and bike set-up and gain nerves of steel.

Prior Mindset and Focus

Relax: this is Zone 1, a skills-based challenge. Be smooth and competent, and the zen of riding will come to you. Focus on feeling your whole body and how you can feel smooth riding. Ignore HR, what power you're doing or if you're in a higher gear than what your friend uses in rollers sessions. Actually, I bet few of your friends use rollers so this can be skill one-upmanship that has a 'cool' factor with huge practical gains.

Warm-Up

- Position yourself between walls of a corridor, in a door frame, between a sofa and a wall – you get the idea.
- Start in an easy gear. If you're still learning, hold onto a firm object with one hand while feeling the balance sensation vary between you balancing and the wall taking your weight.
- Relax – it will come!

Main Session

As the whole session is low to mid-Zone 1 (55–70 per cent HRmax) it can feel like one long relaxed warm-up with no big effort or peak. Your focus during the core of the session depends on your ability, ideally moving on a stage every few weeks/months.

Beginner: look to get time where you can briefly have both hands on the bars and feel like riding properly. It's a leap of faith letting go and balancing but the more you find that balance sweet-spot, the closer to proper roller riding you'll get.

Intermediate: this means you can ride in cycle shoes, in blocks of time on the bars but have the odd wobble or safety 'respite' where you hold onto a firm object and continue pedalling to feel the balance point, but have some weight on the supporting arm. You can vary your hand position on the bars, practise a gear change or two; even try tapping the bottle in its cage. Don't try pulling it out and replacing it: this is for the advanced rider (see below).

Advanced: depending on cycling experience and practice frequency, many riders can get to this stage but it's the product of diligence. At this stage you can ride with few wobble moments, you can take a bottle in and out of the cage, even take things out of your rear cycle pockets. No-handed, one-legged drills or aerobar use really is a very skilled end point for some, not all. At this stage using rollers for warm-ups at races, cool-downs and to practise race-day positioning is possible.

Cool-Down

Just easing into a lower gear allows the light effort to feel very light. As this is an aerobic skill, there is no major time period required to dissipate lactate or to bring the brain back down to normality. Less clothing and equipment to clean up makes this is a quick in-and-out style session.

Post-Session

Though the mileage, top speed and GPS data are all paltry, this session deserves being written up in your diary, especially when you ride continuously for 10 minutes, move over to clipped-in shoes or ride on aerobars for the first time. There are no official roller badges of merit, but you and your diary can know that you're becoming a smoother, more confident rider.

Ways to Advance or Customize

This is the perfect light riding skill session, followed by a shoe change into a run drill. For example, 10 minutes on the rollers, transition, then run with 10 × 50-metre high-knees with jog back recovery, transition, rollers for 8 minutes, and so on through glute-kicks, fast-feet and slow-lunges, etc.

In training many riders use the luxury and comfort of riding on the hoods or tops of a standard handlebar. In racing, however, the tri bar (aka 'aerobar') means higher speed for the same effort and greater relaxation of the upper body between swim and run sections. Tri-bar riding must be practised, or bike handling and the physical stress of the novelty of the position means that, come race-day, the bars go unused or are used sporadically, at best.

There are too many scenarios to list, but if you use your training bike without tri bars for most rides, you must use your race (or training) bike in the tri-bar position at least once a week.

SESSION 6: Tri Position Acclimation or Perfection

Equipment

race bike (*must have tri bars*) or your training bike (*ideally has tri bars*)

cycle shoes
appropriate clothing
helmet

Performance Benefits

Getting your body used to riding on tri bars means you can reap the race-day benefits of more speed, a recovering upper body after the swim and before the run (both of which require upper body input), in addition to reducing the impact of harder head-wind sections which can otherwise sap energy.

Prior Mindset and Focus

If you're new to aerobars and are venturing outside, or you're slightly nervous even after a few seasons of use, choose your route to include quieter sections or dedicated cycle tracks to allow relaxed riding without traffic.

The focus should be on smooth riding. More advanced triathletes can use aerobars for OGE work and high-speed riding, though again, choice of route and safety when riding is paramount.

Warm-Up

- Ride in an easy to moderate gear for the first 15–20 minutes at around 75–85 rpm, moving through low to mid-Zone 1.
- Don't rush to get on the tri bars; let the leg muscles and lower back area warm up thoroughly.

Main Session

This session is all about you growing your confidence, power or speed-handling proficiency. It could be 45 minutes with sections of tri-bar use or a 3-hour endurance ride with big blocks of 20–30 minutes on aerobars.

Use the core of your ride to:

- perfect getting onto and off the tri bars.
- ride smoothly in a straight line on the tri bars.
- steer around subtle bends.
- safely attain higher than normal training speeds while staying relaxed.

And if you are a more advanced triathlete, aim to:

- integrate OGE efforts (as in Session 4) in tri-bar position.
- safely ride on tri-bars above race speed for speed-interval work.

Cool-Down
Riding back home (or for 10–20 minutes, if indoors riding in a light gear) allows your legs to relax.

Post-Session
If the session really works well, like any good time-crunched smart training method, make note of your route, key skills to do and roughly the time it takes – all noted in your **Best Training Sessions** form (see page 220). A lot of riding tri-bars is a no-fireworks, simple skill outcome. Do it, perfect it, but don't overthink it.

Ways to Advance or Customize
As you get more proficient, the use of OGE and above-race-speed riding are key training sessions to progress further. Getting into riding tri-bars throughout the year is the key way to see that you're not just a cyclist but a tri-bar-riding triathlete.

This next session can help you to improve your change times from bike to run.

SESSION 7: Brick Run

Equipment

Indoor/static option:	*Outdoor/advanced:*
a turbo trainer, rollers or gym-bike	tri bike
cycle shoes	helmet
cycle shorts	cycle shoes
running t-shirt	cycle shorts
run shoes	running top
HR belt	run shoes
Garmin device	energy drink bottle
energy drink bottle (*on bike*)	transition rack
towel	
fan (*optional*)	

Performance Benefits

Moving from bike to run differentiates triathletes from pure runners. The more you're able to save energy in shoe-changing, adjust to posture changes and tune into the leg sensations that occur, the better you can run in triathlons. Not every brick needs to be at full-pelt so learn to relax, get used to multiple bike-run changes per session, and mix and match to help winter training boredom.

The simplest of short runs after a longer bike can 'shake out' your muscles and posture, making you feel multi-sport with the smallest change of habit.

You can do a short time trial of 7–12 miles (see www.ctt.org.uk) though holding nothing back, then when you're back to base (or your car) on with your run shoes, try a steady 5k run. It's a baptism of fire, but race-day legs will never feel as bad again.

Prior Mindset and Focus

Think about your ideal outcome: multiple shoe changes with shorter bike run sections to focus on changing rather than effort, or maybe a build-up of steady bike-run, moderate bike-run, hard bike-run.

Are you trying out a new pair of shoes, assessing a run injury by jogging after a bike session, maybe trying to transition from biker to runner as fast as possible with a new dismount strategy and elastic laces? Bricks are varied; very varied.

Warm-Up

Indoors or short bricks:

■ Ride in an easy to moderate gear for the first 10 minutes at around 75–85 rpm, moving through low to mid-Zone 1.

■ Then hop off and run for 5–8 minutes relaxed tempo before returning to your bike.

Longer bike-duration bricks:

■ Warm up as above but don't change back to being a runner, leave your run shoes where you will store your bike after the ride section.

Running off the bike is as much a skill as it is relaxing so nurture your body between disciplines and find ways to save energy as you change clothing.

■ If it's a test run, tell yourself this at the start of the session, rather than get excited mid-ride that you will make it into an awesome brick session.

Main Session

Indoors:

■ Ride for 6–10-minute blocks, mostly in the 85–95 cadence range looking to use aerobars preferably, but focus on smooth aerobic riding

■ If you intend to build your efforts through the session, the first should always be the patient aerobic effort, then build through Zone 2 to possibly Zone 3 by the last effort. For example, a 10-minute bike ride, 6-minute run at Zone 1; 10-second bike, 6-second run at Zone 2 and 10-second bike at Zone 2 with 6-second run into Zone 3.

Outdoors:

- This is best as an endurance ride clocking aerobic miles, but you can incorporate your OGE work for the week; it's fine to do an aerobic ride and follow with an easy run – the brick doesn't have to be intense.
- Use an aerobic 'bike-run, bike-run' sessions outdoors with a bike, and run loop to keep things varied, close to home and never boring – though the neighbours may wonder why you keep coming in and out!

Cool-Down

- Leave some biking, ideally as the last leg loosener (however, if you're doing a short test run to assess injury or muscle soreness, you may finish with a light run).
- Never finish with a maximal run; always add on some spinning to loosen the legs.

Post-Session

Depending on bike and total session duration plus the severity of your run effort, you may need a recovery drink and compression tights or just need to dress, eat and get on with your day. Bricks are not one flavour so adjust your recovery and your next day's sessions depending on how hard things feel today.

Ways to Advance or Customize

Options are infinite but it's important to do some brick training at least once a week. Even some turbo training after a hard run, or a spin on the rollers to warm up for an outside cold run, mean that bricks work in different ways to aid warm up, recovery and transition efficiency. Be clever and you will probably never do just one sport in a session given the option to make it a brick.

This following session will train you to be aware of difficulties and how to cope effectively with them.

Whatever the type of run devised to give 'adversity', it's there to make you better able to deal with race-day fatigue. Take your medicine – it's good for you!

SESSION 8: Run Adversity

Equipment
run shoes
compression socks (e.g. CEP run 2.0 socks)
simple run clothing suitable to the weather conditions
heart monitor
the ability to focus on being a runner with some adversity to deal with

Performance Benefits
Depending on how you achieve run adversity, this will result in a host of varying adaptations:

High Intensity Interval Training (HIIT) – gets you to threshold and above to push the muscular power, lactate clearance and mental toughness. Ultimately, the run is the place where adversity is building and there's nothing afterwards. As you can empty yourself on the run it's worth practising just that.

Double Run Day – this produces fatigued muscles from a morning run in order to challenge your mechanics, muscle soreness and endurance in the second of the day's sessions. As there is no overnight sleep between runs and a working day to get in the way it teaches the mid-long distance triathlete to deal with tired legs while also allowing any time-crunched athlete to split a hard to find long-session into two smaller ones.

Prior Mindset and Focus

Your mind must be telling your legs, 'Get ready for hardship', not reminding you of the run injury that is not getting any better. The focus of this session is on working the legs hard, so be ready or re-think what you can do that day.

Warm-Up

Jog easy for 3–5 minutes – relax: it's not race-day and this is the hardest sport you're about to do. If you can, do some turbo or gym bike riding before you even jog; then go onto 3 minutes progressive effort up to around 75 per cent HRmax. You should feel that you're running smoothly and are warmed up for the core of the session; any serious niggles that are definitely not ready to be hammered need to be listened to at this stage. Don't leave it until it's too late.

Main Session

Hit short: 30–50 minutes

Warm up 8–13 minutes in easy Zone 1; then 5 × 50 metres at 5k race pace; then 1-minute jog recovery to get legs ready for main set speed work.

Main set: 6–8 × 300 metres at best pace to finish all efforts consistently fast.

Allow a full 90-seconds recovery (minimum) to keep the effort consistent: this is best done on a soft running track, smooth grass surface or consistent off-road footpath; keep away from concrete pavement or tarmac.

Cool-Down

Jog easy for 5–10 minutes with relaxed but good tempo running, then (ideally) spin legs on turbo/rollers gym bike for 10 minutes

Hit long: 45–60 minutes
Warm up 8–13 minutes in easy Zone 1, then 5 × 100 metres at 5k pace, and a 400-metre jog recovery

Main set: 7 minutes in low Zone 2, 7 minutes in mid Zone 2, 7 minutes in upper Zone 2/low Zone 3
No recovery between these efforts.

Cool-down: jog easy for 5–8 minutes, then (ideally) spin legs on turbo/rollers/gym bike for 10 minutes

Double Run: Introductory

In the morning: aim for a 40–50 minutes really easy relaxed pace at mid Zone 1, i.e. a nice cruise, ideally before breakfast and with a 40-minute delay afterwards to maximize metabolic training adaptations

In the evening: aim for a 40–50 minutes relaxed run at Zone 1, with 10-second surges to 10k race pace every 5–6 minutes (include 5 minutes jog down at the end)

Double Run: Intermediate

In the morning: aim for a 60–75 minutes run at a really easy relaxed pace at Zone 1 (as above)

In the evening: aim for a 60 minutes run with 15 minutes at an easy pace, $3 \times$ (7 minutes at half marathon pace + 3 minutes RI jog in between), then relaxed running cool-down

Cool-down: as appropriate for each session above, but remember that using your bike to reduce running on already fatigued legs may be the best way to alter your cool-downs.

Post-Session

Running often causes damage to muscles so use of compression tights and a recovery drink (especially if you're tired and don't want to eat straight away) means you get the process of adapting under way faster. Immediate cooling of leg muscles, such as standing in a water butt or outdoor pool may aid heat dissipation and help recovery (especially if it is a warm day).

Ways to Advance or Customize

The HIIT running can be increased in total reps, though the point is to get good at short, sharp efforts that improve your ability to run fast and relaxed, not drag a session beyond its ideal duration.

With the 'Double Run Day' the 2-hour morning run and 1 hour evening run is probably the highest level of stress most age-group athletes will ever absorb and improve with. Any longer and you will be flogging a horse that's already slowing down.

For an Ironman run session idea see this video: http://bit.ly/1PnAyhu.

The following session will help you to get into good shape to tackle hills.

SESSION 9: Hill Economy Efforts

Equipment
cushioned run shoes
run clothing
possibly extra clothing for warm-up and cool-down running

Performance Benefits

Uphill high-intensity running can improve your run efficiency, add to your ability to deal with leg discomfort, and reduce the impact on your muscles. If you are a heavier athlete, this will help you to get an idea of how your weight hinders your movement ability; at the same time, it limits the damage you incur on yourself by using a hard-uphill with soft-downhill approach.

Quick Tip

You need to be in good shape to look for efficiency improvements on top of consistency so this is not a quick fix to cure lack of running. Have a recovery drink in the fridge at the ready if you're going to do some hard effort damage.

Prior Mindset and Focus

You're looking to challenge gravity while keeping composed. This is not about fighting a hill or losing good form. It's effort and good mechanics in one.

A soft surface hill makes damage less likely on jog recoveries, but it can also help those targeting an event where off-road running is part of the final element of the race.

Warm-Up

- Jog easy for 3–5 minutes, then 6–10 minutes progressive effort up to around 80% HRmax, finding your way to the hill you will use.
- If riding a mountain bike or road bike to an ideal location, keep this to less than 20 minutes.
- It is possible to do this session on a treadmill, but outdoor gravity running is a better way to feel the ups and downs.

Main Session

- Choose one of two hill types, either the 'Steep' 15 per cent option or the 'Shallower' 7 per cent option.[1]
- Aim to increase the reps something along the lines of this suggested progression, though ensure your body is getting stronger, not more fatigued or injured, before you commit to doing every week absolutely as described.

A. *Steep reps: over a six-week period progress:*
(1) 8 x 30 seconds (2) 10 x 35 seconds (3) 12 x 40 seconds (4) 12 x 45 seconds (5) 16 x 40 seconds (6)16 x 45 seconds

Each effort is close to maximal with three times as much recovery to jog back down easily (best via a lower gradient route that's a soft surface). For example, the 30 seconds effort has at least 90 seconds recovery jog down.

B. *Shallower incline: over six weeks' progress:*
(1) 4 × 4 minutes; (2) 4 × 5 minutes; (3) 5 × 4.5 minutes; (4) 5 × 5 minutes; (5) 6 × 5 minutes; (6) 7 × 5 minutes.

Again, each effort is close to maximal (> = 90 per cent HRmax) with 1.5 times as much recovery to jog back down easily, e.g. 5 minutes of effort has 7.5 minutes jog recovery.

These are longer recoveries than typical interval sessions, but they cover the practicalities of jogging back down, not rushing and therefore causing injuries from repeated fast downhill running.

Cool-Down

- Relaxed running (or by bike) back home with 10 minutes' light effort straight home.
- Don't aim to add extra endurance onto this session.
- Possibly add on spinning on the turbo trainer to loosen legs.

Quick Tip

Use an energy drink at the top of the hill to keep your throat moist and your blood glucose levels up.

Post-Session

Recovery drink and/or snack with cold shower on legs and change into compression tights.

Ways to Advance or Customize

The maximal sixth week quantity is hard for many age-group athletes to attain. Beyond that there will be little point in trying to add on more. Actually, that should peak form and it's a case of using that fitness in an event, backing off and planning the break-even point that is repeatable most weeks before you once again plan a peak of hill reps. This is not an every week continuous type of session, but one that builds to a peak – plan to peak but also remember to plan when you leave it alone for a while.

Everyone needs to have some idea of how they are doing, so here's a session that gives you a time trial test – just don't do this next session every week!

SESSION 10: Time Trial Test

Equipment
The kit depends on whether you plan to test efficiency if it's an assessment of equipment or if you're entering a single sport event. Bottom line is, you're looking to get some numbers out of this so the session is not just time in the bank. Alternatively, see how it goes if there is a set scenario to observe and quantify.

Performance Benefits
If you test your efficiency it can give a useful insight into how fit you are without pushing yourself to the limit – this makes it more repeatable and turns a humdrum session into a very useful point of reference.

In any discipline, there's nothing like a race against the clock to produce a reality check. At least on the bike you can throw money at the problem of getting faster.

If you're pushing yourself or your equipment in a training session time trial or single-sport event, it means you end up with some data. This will tell you quite how fast you are or how useful the equipment may be. It may say both are wanting but that's why time trials (races) are literally a race of truth.

Prior Mindset and Focus
Be aware of the numbers you're looking at. Is it submax run efficiency, run speed in a 5k or how much a set of race wheels takes off your usual training loop time? You may be able to 'guesstimate' end results but not make your mind up in a binary yes/no manner. Data

often takes a few plots to be able to make assessments of methods, kit choices and overall triathlon ability. Be clear in your process, but open to the outcomes.

Warm-Up

A warm-up of 10–15 minutes is probably best for any test. Be it a session at 80 per cent maximum for run efficiency over 3 miles or for a time trial over 10 miles in an aerobic position, build up enough time to be mentally and physically ready to do your planned session. If it is a time trial, spending 1–2 minutes at threshold to begin the process of lactate turnover is useful towards the end of your warm up.

Main Session

The Submax: Continuous 20–40 minutes at 80 per cent of maximum HR (top Zone 1) Don't aim for a set pace. Instead, work at the desired HR and aim to relax your body to get most efficiency out of your limited effort input. You go as fast as staying at 80 per cent allows. This could be a 3-mile section of a run or a long climb on the bike.

From this, you'll get a time, an average HR, and an idea of how efficient this makes you (or the equipment you're testing). You can repeat this the next day or next week to assess how repeatable and accurate your testing methods are.

The Race of Truth: Bottom line, this is you against the clock. You give it your very best effort and the numbers are the numbers. You may be faster in warmer weather, with different wheels or if you had a good night's sleep. However, this is the truth of the matter: distance, time and what you learned about pacing. Examples include 400-metre pool swim efforts, open-water Ironman swim races, 10-mile time trials, the local Strava hill climb, 5k park run or spring half-marathon.

You should not overdo these – they are examples of high-intensity effort so they need to be done when you're in good health, consistent in training, and looking to add some sharpening to your triple sport plans.

Cool-Down

Keep this functional to dissipate heat but do not extend or look to make up for a poor outcome. Use this time to assess what the numbers tell you, how well you executed the process, and what it means for any changes in your training, nutrition or tech use. It's a series of numbers to use constructively, not to deny or make excuses about.

Post-Session

Recover in such a way that you come away from the effort feeling like from beginning to end of process you did everything the right way. Don't dwell on bad outcomes or overly shout about good ones – just log it and make changes over the next few days and weeks to improve on what the data said you need to improve upon.

Ways to Advance or Customize

The key with any time trial or test is to do it in a planned and repeated manner to allow you to confirm the data and absorb the 'knowledge' you need to make changes for the better. A test is not the outcome: it's what that says about your good and bad habits, good and bad equipment – even good and bad testing methods. So, use the data to direct your next action. If anything is not good enough ('My 5k is too slow') it may just be telling you the truth about your lack of training consistency, or it could be saying that that's your limit, or close to it, so well done for getting that close to your best. Just *wanting* to be faster does not mean you can always *get* faster.

Remember: data empowers positive actions to hopefully improve future data.

The Ten Worst Sessions – and Why

There is a logic that seems to say that as long as it's called training it must be for the good of the athlete. It must be a good use of time and not a wasted effort – it's called training, so it stands to reason it is causing improvement, right? Wrong!

The very fact that you step out of your door with some sports attire on doesn't mean what you're about to do is going to make you any better at that sport, that the energy used is going to help you perform at a higher level, or that it will be better than staying at home. Training (or should we say 'doing an activity in some way?') does not mean it's a useful training stimulus to help you to become better.

Here are my pet peeves, which not only waste valuable time and energy, but can perpetuate a macho mentality, exercise addiction tendencies and periods of ill-health.

1 **The Group Steady Session that's become a Race:** This is going off-plan by doing *no one's* plan. It's what happens when you get competitive people all in one place at one time, with no clear leader. The session starts sedately (if you're lucky) and gradually gets faster. Some athletes may be doing what was advertised as a steady session, meanwhile many are racing in a stealthy way: they try, but are trying not to look like they are trying. The end result is a lack of a clear zone outcome. They are all over the place: from a Zone 1 that creeps into a Zone 3, to another that may be all Zone 2 yet believes it was 'steady'. No one attached a number; the efforts were not clearly defined in the way that an interval session should be; and worst still, almost everyone is part of the problem because they are not the solution to the big issue – the lack of respect for one another in a session that has no leader.

Many moan about these types of sessions; a few get demoralized enough to give up as a result; and plenty believe that because it's what they've always done (and the odd fast person may turn up) that it's the right way to do things.

Solution: Have clear group session aims/varying levels of ability and, if not, train on your own or with like-minded people away from the madness.

2 **The Test Myself (because I Feel Good):** This has the beginnings of a logical process of good training: testing yourself to see where you are at, what you can take, and what is a realistic time-frame to be at peak fitness. However, the randomness of the timing ('I feel good') means either you are looking for good data, possibly feeling good so thinking it must be time to work hard (and then feel bad afterwards), or you have just had a random thought that a time trial is always a good idea.

Tests, if done randomly, fail to be of much use. To get useful performance data you need to plan when you will test yourself and how often to repeat the test (e.g. every six weeks). Feeling good halfway through a session is no logic to thinking that a time trial or similar effort is warranted or even useful. These hammer-fests are usually, deep down, when you ask in-depth questions, actually the result of a lack of confidence in ability and so they aim to help you feel better about yourself. I get it. I know all athletes have a streak of insecurity.

Solution: Plan your significant races against the clock; otherwise, feel fine with finishing sessions without always being wasted or 'needing' to hit Zone 2 and Zone 3.

3 **The Rushed Session that Makes You Stressed – Throughout:** If the third rule of Fit Club is to warm up properly, this is the antithesis. Warming up prepares your body and brain for a session. Jumping straight in and going for it is a stress akin to our caveman ancestors being scared by something and running at a moderate intensity for a long time. We didn't do that: we sprinted for a short distance to chase food or to stop being something else's food. We also trekked at a slow pace to hunt and gather. We did not do threshold or close to it for an hour to find food. If we had done, we would be as dead as a dodo.

So that commute that starts fast as you're late for work, or the ride that starts quick because someone's already warmed up and is also amped-up on caffeine – well, these and many other rushed starts to training just stress you out, create lactate too early in the session, and leave you mentally unable to relax, so avoid them.

Solution: If at all possible leave time to warm up for sessions: allow 10+ minutes. Similarly, warm up before group sessions that start quite fast so your body is ready for the increase in pace. If rushed, try to build into the rush to work; slower earlier on will mean you can stay slightly more aerobic. If you're a bit late just explain that 'Coach Joe Beer doesn't want me to go anaerobic'.

4 **Training When You're Tired (Really Tired):** It was the faces of the people who sat in on a Q&A session with Scott Neyedli during a training camp in Lanzarote that made me chuckle to myself. It was when he said that sometimes he would just turn around and go home, even if he'd got as far as the changing rooms of the pool but was still feeling too tired. They were sceptical. Then they realized that he was deadly serious: if he was not up for a session, what was the point in spending another ninety minutes getting even more exhausted? Many would think an Ironman winner must do every session, especially if they were already at the pool. Many of the audience would have done the swim and been worse for it. Hence, it's junk to train if you're too tired.

On race-day, whatever the distance, you have tapered down your training, you're fresh (or you damned well should be) and your muscles are glycogen-stocked for action. So training need not be constantly in a state of fatigue. Sometimes the best session is no session whatsoever. None. Nil. Zero. Zilch. Go home, eat, get to bed. Listen to your body.

Solution: Look for signs of wavering motivation and fatigue. When you're so tired it's hard to even get started you may want to bail out and start again the next day. Just don't roll missed training over to the next day – it's a session that is lost to history now (at least, with an outcome that's positive).

Within your swim sessions incorporate some haul-outs to transform them from pure swims into triathlon reality where you have to exit the water and run to your bike (not hang off the lane rope hyperventilating).

5 **Training Extra because You Have Some Spare Time:** I love training. It's been a part of who I am for over thirty – gulp! – years. I have had almost unlimited time to barely any spare time and all the possible different amounts in between these two extremes. Yet given an increase in time I would always build training, not go into excessive overload straight away. It just made sense, yet many given some extra hours will just train based on the 'more-is-better' philosophy. If you have extra time to get a session on your to-do list done and guaranteed for the week, good. However, just rushing out the door with no plan except to 'just do some training' is an exercise addict's compulsion.

Solution: Have a plan for a week or fortnight that deals with the sessions you really need to get done – the ones that are regulars and the bonus ones on top. Use extra time if you get some to do the bonus sessions or, better still, the admin that keeps your kit, racing entries and life in order, e.g. have you got your bikes insured for training and racing? (If not, see www. pedalcover.co.uk for details.)

6 **Ill, But Still Do it Anyway:** The people who push through an illness are pushing their luck. Once you're so ill that every-day functioning is hard, training 'plans' should back off to healthy 'mode'. If you can barely stay awake, breathe without coughing, walk without limping and so on, perhaps you need to cancel that session or race as it's a bridge too far. I understand some massive races need to be done when you're far from 100 per cent or you will miss a once-in-a-lifetime chance. For the other 99 per cent of instances, get well first then train or race later.

Let's try to be healthy and vibrant before sessions, shall we? Ill or injured athletes hobbling out to train are doing themselves no good.

Solution: Be really honest with yourself as to how well you are and what good the planned session or race will actually add to your knowledge, fitness and confidence. If the answer is very little, adjust the plan and look to get healthy as your immediate goal.

7 **Carrying On for the Full One Hour:** Who actually said that sessions need to be exactly one hour in length? It was not an exercise physiologist. In fact, it probably stems from swim lanes being booked for an hour or the fact that most working day activities are packaged into an hour. Meetings are usually half an hour or a 'full-hour', then there's the 'lunch hour' and planners on your smartphone which have defaults of schedules lasting an hour. However, the only endurance events I know of that last sixty minutes are the hour records for cycling (>56 km in aero position) and running (>21 km). There is no swimming hour record recognized by FINA. Oh, and there's the Concept 2 ergo hour record (>18 km).

Not every session you do as training has to stretch to an hour. If technique is waning in the pool, get out before the sixty minutes is up (and here many coaches could do their athletes a favour by grabbing them out early on occasion). If you're having to ride around in circles to complete your hour ride, why not try a longer route next time? And if you run on the spot to ensure you clock sixty minutes before going through the front door, it's time to take a chill pill. In a taper week or when adaptation is the reason for training, give yourself the option to stop when stopping feels right.

Solution: Think about training sessions as having a goal and question if sometimes you need to stop when you're done – you could achieve the desired outcome in under one hour or any other integer of hours. Train on 'feel-for-time' rather than to the exact sixty minute countdown timer. A two-hour ride might be done in 1 hour 48 minutes or 2 hour 9 minutes – be honest, not pedantic.

8 **Running London because You Have a Summer Ironman:** No training study or any bulk of athlete experiences I have shows that an April marathon will help your summer Ironman. There, I've said it. So get

over London as the stopping point for every wannabe Ironman athlete. There are far more effective April sessions for you to be doing.

Solution: Look at the specificity of Ironman (running 26 miles with tired legs, starting at least six hours in) and realize that being a stronger biker, perfecting feeding while cycling, and optimizing your pacing are central to being Ironman-ready. You have to have long runs, but it's economical strong running, not fast stand-alone marathon running, that's the key.

9 **Doing a Session Just because a Fast Person Does it:** We can learn from what the elites do. They set the highest levels of workmanship. However, their age, genes, training experience, and support network are second to none – we cannot just copy. There are principles to adhere to, ways to progress the session, and key elements to maximize improvement. The eventual goal of training is not for everyone to be doing what Scott Molina, Chrissie Wellington, Spencer Smith or any of the greats found was their best training session, week or 'block'. That worked for *them*, at that stage in *their* career, and with nothing but training outcomes to think about.

Solution: Read what the elites do, at professional and age-group level, but look for how the article/interview adapts this to people who aren't elites and see what you can do to learn from them. Tweak their training ideas and sessions to suit *your* needs – to make a plan of what *you* intend to do. It will still be better than just making things up as you head out the front door.

10 **That Last Big Session that Breaks the Bank:** Whether it's race week or the last stage of a key training block, be sure that you don't break yourself with that one last extra session. You may have lost some sessions and want to make up for it – but sorry, that's not how physiology works. You can't just pile up missed sessions or suddenly add extra on top of an already peaking physiological system. Detailed research shows us that adding 2 per cent on top of a 90 per cent interval doesn't make it better, going from 3 milligrams/kilogram to 6 milligrams/kilogram doesn't make caffeine ergogenic, and increasing Zone 2 training

from <5 per cent to >20 per cent reduces fitness improvements. Always trying to do more or extra is not the point of a plan. Plans ideally build in progression, recovery, flexibility or training load and learn what best works for an athlete. More is not better; more refined and personalized to *you* is better.

To train well, you must sleep well. Naps and a good night's sleep are the ways to make your training feel turbocharged.

Solution: Plan your key training blocks – the biggest days, the longest sessions. However, most importantly define adaptation weeks, exactly tapering workload into your A-races and a last race of the season which is followed by time 'off-plan'.

Use the **My Best Training Sessions** form in Appendix 2 (see page 220) to log sessions that go really well – and look through these regularly to remind yourself of your successes and to learn from them.

BE TIME-EFFICIENT – THE EASY WAY

- I bring gym/ indoor cycling shoes with me wherever I am travelling in the UK or abroad. There is always a gym nearby and, although I am not a big fan of 'gym bikes', there is a good chance you will be staying at a hotel or close to a gym where they have a proper stationary bike.
- I like to listen to audio books to maximize time when training indoors.
- Treadmill running is a great tool for measured running and will reduce the likelihood of injuries especially compared to running on concrete or tarmac.
- I don't measure every session – I know some people who won't train unless they have a 'computer' of some description. Seems crazy to me as I rarely measure any session. Especially for easy runs and bikes. Try to smell the flowers and enjoy 'being'.
- As athletes we are often highly self-critical and Type A characters. Sometimes our mood or happiness is conditional on whether we have had a good training session or race. Be grateful that we are in the minority of people who are able to do these incredible multisport activities.
- Resting, when you're overreached or tired, is the best training session you can do for improving your performance.

LEE PIERCY FATHER, *fast learner and fast – very fast – Powerman Arizona 2015 winner and World Champion Age Group duathlete (and occasional triathlete)*

CHAPTER SIX

Achieving Strength Effectively

To gain strength you need patience, effort and nutrients.

This chapter is like good strength training: short, precise and with no fluff. Look at the training plans of most professional endurance athletes and you'll see some strength work. It may be pre-hab, re-hab or in addition to training with resistance in sessions, but it's clear that just doing endurance work does not automatically add strength. When once upon a time athletes would shun weights out of a fear of becoming 'muscle bound' or female athletes 'bulking-up', it's now clear that resistance work, if done consistently, aids performance ability, offsets muscle-loss with ageing (called 'sarcopenia'), and may well help with injury prevention. Be aware though: doing bonkers things with kettle bells, overloading a squat rack, or jumping into resistances where you left off two months ago *will* cause you injury, so avoid!

Hard intervals for 4 to 10 minutes are the speed 'icing' on the aerobic base 'cake'. They work to add that all-important final 10 per cent.

More and more endurance training may well get you to the finishing line aerobically efficient, but you will probably not get there the fastest that you could. You would have plenty of endurance reserves for next time, but lack being 'faster' on the day.

To go faster, ultimately you need more power rather than just lots of endurance. It is possible to add more power/speed with intervals – and a rough review of literature would say maybe 5–9 per cent could be added by a short-term high-intensity-training (HIIT) programme – such as 3–6 weeks of, say, 6 × 4 minutes interval. There have been some direct strength training studies that show that training in the gym the right muscles for your chosen sport may well improve performance – it rarely shows that you can make it a whole lot worse.

There is an argument for strength training as a health benefit: it puts stresses across muscles that may not get used. This is very useful if you stop running and just swim and bike. It does take time, and you're reading this because you want to make the most of your time. However, there are several – well, many – solutions to integrate strength training:

1 Get a home gym – as simple as some free weights to a host of machines and the necessary mirror that all gyms seem to need.
2 Integrate gym work with additional low impact swim skill or deep-water running sessions under one roof.
3 Drop one session a week of your strongest sport and focus on muscular strength in weak and less used muscle groups that you need for triathlon.
4 Add body-weight work exercises (e.g. dips, press-ups and squats) after, say, run and bike sessions to sneak some additional resistance work into that time slot.
5 Make added resistance a part of your aerobic sessions (see below).

First Rule: Patience

Strength training is a long-term, gradual accumulative effect – just like any other training. You're adding cells, waiting for gains to add to gains … so it takes time. If you don't stick to plans, then don't start in the first place – instead, go and swim, bike and run. We need consistency and diligence, not sporadic sessions, resistances and exercises.

You may need to fall back onto an 'on-the-road option', which can be a strength, a step back into the history of exercise machines, or the realization that some stretch 'cordz' needs to be packed on every business trip. In your hotel room resistance exercises may seem bizarre right now, but it can be a life-saver when you feel like you're losing strength and the options for strength work are zilch.

Though you could do very light intro-ductory work I would suggest not planning to add a sudden strength training regime in the middle of the racing season. Unless you need some serious rehab strength work, wait a while. Think about the off-season as a great time to get energy into working out the best resources to use, getting organized (clipboard, gym gear, etc.), and starting a whole body plan at a conservative point.

Second Rule: Effort!

There is no one special exercise, no one special sets, or reps, or rest sequence. Resistance training (let's move away from 'gym work' or 'weights') is about logical progression, whole-body thinking and specific focus where there is the need based on an injury or known weak-nesses. You may want to get various experts to suggest muscles and exer-cises you want to concentrate on. It's not the same for everyone, though clearly everyone uses a fairly similar set of muscles to swim, bike or run.

In all the strength training research I have read, it does not talk about the gym drivel you have probably heard at many gyms, namely that you need to:

Rowing is a brilliant way to warm up for weight training and, as it uses many of your tri muscles, it can be a useful indoor, winter, cross-training session.

- do 3 × 12–15 reps
- rush the rest between sets (or exercises)
- be in the gym for an hour, or more

Speaking with some of the best strength training experts in the UK, they say get in, work hard, get out. It's not endurance training, it's *strength* work, so quality is high and time-length of the session is not long.

Though you cannot just throw in maximal efforts, it seems that 8-repe-tition maximum (8 RM), or when rep number nine cannot happen due to muscular fatigue – well, that appears to be hard enough to cause significant

Recovery drinks work to get essential nutrients into your body when you are fatigued and lack appetite. The session has to be hard or very long to justify using these drinks. They are emphatically *not* treats.

strength gain, but is not so risky that you injure yourself trying to get these excessive resistances moved (e.g. 4 RM).

Every session needs to have a warm-up moderate effort 12 rep set, to get the exercise coordinated in muscle and mind, then move to 8 RM. As this will probably peak in effectiveness after 6–8 weeks, it's better to build from 12 RM, 10 RM and eventually 8 RM, peaking sometime in late winter or early spring. This is then complemented by early season efforts and resistance work – you move the strength out of the gym and into the sports themselves.

Third Rule: Nutrients Rule!

That is, strength training requires sufficient nutrition to create the right anabolic environment. You don't want to enter sessions really hungry, eat little afterwards, or ignore the need for quality protein in the diet. While many triathletes are carbohydrate savvy, they fail to have quality protein in their diet at high enough levels to support muscular adaptation, help gene messaging turn training into an adaptation, and support an immune system that is getting challenged on a daily basis.

If you are a long-term vegetarian (and I was once one myself so this is not veggie-bashing), you may respond particularly well to a short-term creatine monohydrate

Quick Tip

Aim to consume 25 grams of quality protein very close to any hard resistance training sessions – this could be a pre-session protein bar/flapjack, a whey protein shake during a session, or a tuna salad soon after. This is a building block to assist protein gains in the muscle tissue, but also aids getting messages around the body to trigger genes to do their stuff.

loading phase. Taking 5 grams once a day with a carbohydrate source (e.g. in orange juice at breakfast) for one month will bring your muscle stores back up to an even playing field with your meat-eating competitors. It may be a 'suck-it-and-see' approach, but vegetarians have been shown to have low resting levels of creatine in the muscle, and raising creatine does increase strength. Though anecdotal, I have seen veggies get stronger and recover better when doing occasional creatine loading phases (e.g. every 3–4 months).

You may increase your total 'lean' mass due to greater glycogen storage creatine loading (see above) and slight increases in muscle tissue. However, weight training should not increase fat mass, but instead make your musculature better at delivering power. Dropping fat is more of a focus than worrying that lean mass gains have made you heavier. More muscle burns more calories, even at rest, so fat reserves should be chipped away at, not added too.

For simple ways to get the most from your strength training, see the tips here.

Quick Tip

Vary the order, focus and exercises from time to time – but don't throw in anything too varied or you're likely to get injured. *Remember:* logical progression, not random confusion.

Quick Tip

Have a clipboard plan to keep resistances progressive – a muscle must be challenged to cause a significant adaptation (see the Resistance Training Diary on page 222).

Quick Tip

Use an mp3 player to get focused in your warm-up and be mindful when training; wearing ear buds or headphones signals to others that you're training.

Drinks like PowerBar Charger are designed to give you a boost during high-intensity training sessions and races, and provide you with a caffeine kick and other ergogenics to get the highest effort out of your body.

Quick Tip

Plan your nutrition to get calories, quality protein (see above) and consistent energy levels as you approach training sessions – resistance training needs nutrition; it's not instead of.

Quick Tip

Blend the gym resistance training into the programme of three-sport training to get the best effect. It may take some testing of what days suit you best to do your gym training.

Strength Training for You

Having an idea of your total mass, fat mass and lean mass can give you a real idea of how your training changes your body composition.

Some triathletes never do strength training and they are still very effective. The fact that they are naturally strong, are not injury prone and they don't stress about not going to the gym seems to work for them. They may take it up as they get older and need extra strength work and something new (and indoors) to do.

If you already have a high lean mass (mesomorphs), you must be wary of too much strength training – to increase further mass may look good on the beach, but will hinder you as a three-sport person. At the end of the day – well, at the end of a race – you still need to be a runner, not a bodybuilder. Gaining muscle is hard for anyone; no one actually looks at weights and gains muscle. It's just that some people gain a sense of their muscle size and store more glycogen/water (not sure which) after doing resistance training. If in doubt, ask other athletes what they think of your training, body type, needs, and weaknesses, and their comments will probably point to the direction your training in the gym needs to go.

Use your **Weight Training** form in Appendix 2 (see page 221) to record key data about your strength training using weights.

CHAPTER SEVEN

Eat Right, Run Better

I have been a PowerBar user since the early 1990s. My first-ever article in *Two Twenty Triathlon* magazine, about sports nutrition, shows me running over the famous iron bridge at Ironbridge during the 1991 Marathon (Ironman) triathlon – the first year Hawaii Ironman qualification ever took place on UK soil. Long before that, before I even knew about sports nutrition, I would mix bicarbonate of soda with orange juice, then crack off a fast run around my home village. This was a time of experimentation: the days of glucose tablets underneath sweat bands for long runs; of liquefying my whole supper in a blender to see if this made it easier to consume and aid recovery (for the record – no, it didn't, and it tasted foul); and eating lots of beetroot before a half marathon. Alas, I was not a nitrate genius twenty years ahead of the current nitrate-loading bonanza. I didn't then know that beetroot contains nitrates; it was just that my dad was a great gardener and I loved beetroot too much – I must have had one of the earliest cases of beetroot-trots and pink-urine, as documented in a 1990 training diary!

You name a sports nutrition (legal!) supplement and I have probably read about it into the early hours, used it many times over, and experienced its ups and downs. Nutritional ergogenics, that is, dietary actions and products that improve performance, should be of interest to you as well. You're in a sport where diet is a key factor in your performance so use this knowledge to your advantage, or abuse it to your disadvantage.

I was very well aware that sports nutrition can make a difference when used correctly before many would give it credit. In the very early 1990s I was using a glucose polymer drink, sourced from a hospital by a top coach and physiologist. This was being supplied to top cyclists to keep energy levels up on longer rides and to aid recovery. While many still used water and malt loaf – or just water – I had this 'Maxijoule' to fuel training and my

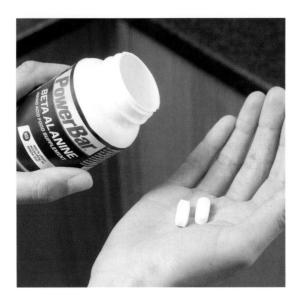

High performance ergogenics like Beta Alanine may improve performance, but many are beyond the needs of most athletes, so focus on the essentials that provide the greatest gain.

Quick Tip

Stock and keep track of the basics you need in sports nutrition terms: energy drink powder, zero calorie hydration tabs, recovery drink and low-dose multivitamin.

early Ironman races. It just made hydration, consistent energy and natural stops in training all better controlled. I product-tested creatine monohydrate, invented a glycerol-loading drink, and had some of our best Ironman athletes using L-Carnitine – all long before these became mainstream.

Today, however, we no longer need to know the importer of a product or be able to plug into what the professionals are getting. Sports nutrition is abundant and many mid- and long-course races provide it in bucketfuls on the big day. The internet and complex distribution networks all over the globe mean we have access to products designed for endurance performers. So we also need to use knowledge to get the most from something still considered by many to be between fairly insignificant to tantamount to cheating. It's neither.

As you train and race you will lose fluid faster than sedentary people – listen to your thirst.

Start with What You Eat

Training happens for probably 300 to 800 hours per year. Competitions probably amount to just 5 per cent of this time. In fact, recent trade surveys put it at 350 hours and 4 to 8 hours (or 1–2 per cent), respectively. So, while the impact of training is meant to make racing better, the use of nutrition in training sessions can amount to an improvement many times greater than that from using it in racing alone. To put it another way: we know nutrition can help your races, but what about the other 250 to 350 days when you're training – surely this is a priceless place to make use of nutrition? Why leave this daily part of your life to be just normal instead of it being an ergogenic. If, as the saying goes (and it's 100 per cent true) that you are what you eat, why leave sports nutrition just for race-day?

You don't need complicated analysis of nutrients using scales, tables and an attention to food that takes all the fun out. This can trigger some nasty and long-lasting negative food associations. After all, this is your hobby; something to make you more rounded, not more neurotic or inflexible about food choices. I need to state it right now but the in-vogue 'paleo' diet, specific fruit juices, mineral supplements or specialist regimes will not make a tail-end Charlie into a podium contender. So find your dietary sweet spot and see food beyond just good, bad or 'what a triathlete eats'.

Granny knew best – unprocessed foods really are the basis for keeping yourself fit and recovering well.

RIGHT NOW!

Take a sample of your diet using the **Food Diary** (see page 217). I would start now. Yes, backdate to yesterday, remembering everything you ate, or this morning if you have a bad memory (or it's a particularly bad day to start on).

This not only shows how hard it is to recall, honestly, the last twenty-four hours accurately, but it may also show that every day is similar because recall is close to immediate. Add training type, quality of session and any positive or negative experiences in the session as part of this food diary. Make a diary note to come back to this page, and put a bookmark here – you have some scribbling to do!

Simple Diet Makeover

With this random three days of food intake ahead of you, first do the following:

■ **Look at the variety of foods** – is it a very repetitive, narrow spectrum of nutrients you're taking in, or eclectic and varied? Using the **Food Diary** form in Appendix 2 (see page 217) jot down some alternative foods that you like that you could fit in where monotony is taking over.

Action: Now add these to your weekly shopping list and try shopping in some different shops

■ **Look at the timing of eating** – we don't run on clockwork, to the same pattern as the next person or even the same every day. Do you tend to eat at fixed times, grab it when you can, or do you time things to enable work and training to be well fuelled? Is it planned or last-minute?

Action: Add more planning of food preparation or make time in your diary for eating properly in your normal day. This is especially important if work, family or training always tend to make you poor at putting your food quality high on the list of priorities.

■ **Look at training responses** – did you have sessions that were affected by poor eating? Do you fail to eat after training due to restricting calories? Do you eat poorly or very little when not training?

Action: Add reminders to ensure you plan nutrition before, during and after training. I don't wish to uncover big food issues. (If these exist, see a specialist via a referral from your GP.) However, some tweaks to your timing and association between food and training can reap big rewards in energy and training outcomes.

So this simple three-day diet diary can lead you to make small tweaks to your diet. You must like what you eat and be able to continue the process for weeks and months – it's a change for the best, for the long haul. I would suggest this happens anything from once a month to once every three months. Just be sure to include weekdays and weekends; don't tell yourself when you're about to start this check-up. That way you immediately have to backdate twenty-four hours so you're reporting on yourself before you have time to change things. Be honest and you will gain a lot from this exercise.

If you truly know that your diet has a big bearing on your weight, not being what you're happy with or causing lacklustre performances, then make dates in your personal diary to check on your diet, now! Taking charge of your food intake when working, at weekends and when racing is just as big a time-crunch challenge as getting to the pool or finding time to do all the races you would like to do.

What's the Opposite of Ergogenic?

Few people know what the things are that make them worse performers. This enemy of going faster is called (cue drum roll) an *ergolytic*. The very belief that something could make you worse is already having a bearing on your performance – you know the person who says the gel they've just eaten will cause stomach ache or that chocolate bar yesterday is making them less fit? It's fair enough to have an opinion, but true ergolytics are the things that we really do need to keep at arm's length, especially when trying to build up to events that demand a lot of us or which are at the limits of our endurance. At these times we have few reserves to squander, therefore little point to be packing on the lard.

The rule of 'what-the-hell' seems to take over when we look at some athletes' behaviour towards ergolytics. That is, one ergolytic seems to lead to another. Good nudges us into more good. Bad makes us say, 'Oh, what the hell!' The list below (not all nutritional habits) has been built up over time, for the most part it's common sense or builds on news pieces you have probably heard in the media already.

It is hard to put an exact percentage drop in performance to any of these ergolytics. A small or infrequent occurrence is unlikely to have any effect unless the athlete subsequently worries about 'not being perfect'. Where something becomes excessive or detrimental is a very, very hard thing to define – though I think we all know, for example, that a 'skinful' of alcohol is not going to make us better at triathlon and is likely to end in injury, or over-eating and, if happening regularly, should be delved beneath for reasons and ways to be controlled before they can damage a supposedly fit exterior.

Here is my Top Ten of ergolytic 'naughties':

1. Excessive alcohol, stimulants or self-prescribed pain medicines.
2. Highly-refined sugars and quick 'highs', fatty snacks.
3. Overly processed and refined foods with poor nutrient content; poor key nutrient intake of iron, quality protein, slow-release carbohydrates.
4. Hydrogenated or trans-fats (e.g. pies, biscuits, cakes); over-consumption.
5. Pollution (e.g. smoke, chemicals, electrical equipment/lines and carbon monoxide).
6. Over-stressed by work or life events, poor sleep and inability to relax.
7. Excessive competing in technique and endurance-building sessions.
8. Aggressive training progression despite body breakdown and/or professionals, such as physios, warning of the situation.
9. Mega-doses of antioxidants in an attempt to make up for poor eating or reduce muscle damage or illness.
10. Treating training and racing as your second job, and as such getting far too obsessed about every meal, supplement use and straying into banned substance use.

Knowing your enemy – alcohol, excessive calories, caffeine or takeaways – is half the battle. Perhaps you never have a takeaway for fear of it 'being bad' or think more is better with vitamins and supplements? You shouldn't look to live like a monk and be perfect in every way – it's too stressful. This was my biggest lesson in growing up: the reality is nothing 100 per cent good or bad.

Instead, try to find foods that make you feel good, look good (leaner, perhaps) and help your energy levels in training sessions. That's not trying to eat boiled rice as you ride or thinking pool water consumed accidentally during a swim session is enough for hydration purposes. If an action in your diet appears weird, illogical and has no factual basis, then it may be best to limit its occurrence.

A travelling lunchbox is a great way to control the majority of your food intake and helps you to avoid having to buy expensive and poor quality processed items on the road.

RIGHT NOW!

Look again at your diet diary or maybe a previous training log you kept during a period of concentrated training. How are you with the ergolytics nutrition and otherwise? Perhaps you need to revisit your SWOT and add a 'Threat' or 'Weakness' that you had not realized before?

The EFSA Effect

As sports nutrition has grown to a multi-billion pound industry, it has in some cases resulted in a lack of quality control, use of banned ingredients or just benefits claimed on adverts and labels impossible to achieve. Since 2010 the European Food Standards Agency (http://www.efsa.europa.eu)

has looked at various sports nutrition product ingredients, supplements and dietetic products. It has, with whatever evidence has been presented to it, been giving directives on products and usage.

It is, however, not without its shortcomings. In some cases recent sports nutrition research known to many has been omitted, the directive is very conservative on its suggested use or lacks vision to translate to scenarios that you, the endurance athlete, experience which an EU panel will probably never experience. For example, you know that a sports drink (or gel and water, for that matter) during a hard, hot race can bring you around and make the finishing line come a lot faster and easier. Yet one conclusion of an EFSA report (http://www.efsa.europa.eu/en/efsajournal/pub/2211.htm) states that the panel 'concludes that a cause and effect relationship has not been established between the consumption of carbohydrate-electrolyte solutions and reduction in rated perceived exertion/effort during exercise.' Think of that one 2, 5, 10 or 16 miles into the longest triathlon you have ever done – no brainer!

The EFSA effect has been, and will continue to be, that some of the bogus and exaggerated claims by some manufacturers will be banned. Some products will shuffle off the shelves never to be seen again. In fact, adverts in the UK have already been changed and products have been tweaked. Did you notice a change in labels in 2012 or thereabouts? Whatever the tweaking that EFSA does to supplements and sports nutrition products, there are some proven ways to supplement your diet, add logical daily tips for nutrition use and to improve your daily training activities. It need not add much time to your training preparation, but if it gives you an extra 1 to 2 or even 3 per cent improvement, then it's a time-crunch benefit.

Fasting or Frugal?

Training the first thing after waking up and without eating or drinking any calories is commonly termed 'fasted training'. This empty stomach feeling, when combined with morning ablutions before you go out the door, gives you the feelings of training 'light'. Inside, your body's insulin levels are low and your body is using stored carbohydrate in the liver to trickle-feed the bloodstream. There will be (and must be!) carbohydrate stored in the muscles from the foods eaten in previous days.

A little-known fact is that there are fat droplets stored alongside your muscle fibres which can be used as fuel during low to moderate levels of training. When you use these intramyocellular-triacylglycerol (IMTG) in a fasted session, they can be used to the greatest extent possible because carbohydrate feeding has not suppressed their use. Maybe as much as 250–500 calories per hour can come from IMTG, saving your muscle carbohydrate (called glycogen), and therefore increasing endurance.

Be warned, though! Training fasted over excessive durations can cause your body a fair degree of stress to the immune system. Most advocates say between one and two hours is enough, probably once or twice a week at most for the amateur athlete. The IMTGs themselves actually may drop 40 to 60 per cent during the session. However, the best way for them to be restored is probably to wait to have food for around 40 minutes after the session. Don't hit the recovery drink or Frosties when you get home; let the IMTGs restore themselves while you shower, change and get that healthy slow-release breakfast ready. At time-crunch triathlete speed, of course.

Here's a session you can follow to help you train your muscles to use their internal fat stores more efficiently. Use the evening before to ready your equipment. Be sure any others doing the ride know you will be fasted; no racing and don't look to pig out after the session in a café binge. It can be a run, bike or rowing session or similar aerobic activity. Indoors or out.

A Proven Endurance Session to Stimulate Fat Use

Benefits: improved efficiency to use, store and train the muscles' internal fat (IMTG) stores – helping save glycogen.

Start time: anything from 6 a.m. for the early birds to 9.30 a.m. for the later risers. However, don't start this session fasted after 10.30 a.m. as this will be too stressful on your body.

Warm-Up: first 10–20 minutes relaxed, keep the effort controlled (<70 per cent HRmax), the terrain/resistance easy.

A morning training session without breakfast can help to keep your body tapping into its thrifty gene to make it more efficient at using fat and storing fat within the muscle while making sessions more comfortable.

Main session: HR around 65–80 per cent HRmax – this is all about fluid effort, enjoying the low to moderate effort and teaching your muscles to use the internal fats by not going too hard. You may sip on water or zero calorie sports drink.

Cool-down: make the last 5–10 minutes easy; spin small chain ring, jog steady or reduce rowing stroke rate and effort. No recovery drink, instead wait 40 minutes before having breakfast or brunch.

This next session not dissimilar to the fasted session (see A Proven Endurance Session to Stimulate Fat Use, above), but there are a few key differences to help you if you notice that when you do a fasted session you tend to get very tired or increase your chances of illness. If this sounds like you, try the following session.

Low-Cal or Later Cal?

Start fasted, do a short period with no food intake, but then trickle-feed a small amount of calories to boost your immune function and post-session wellness.

Once you break your fast you switch your muscles onto using very slightly more carbohydrate in training. This is not a good–bad switch where you must always try to train fasted in order to be 'good'. However, sometimes starting a session fasted makes sense because:

1 It's easier to get out the door than to eat, wait and then eventually (most likely now in a rush) to start your session slightly stressed and looking to make up time to get to work, to meet a group or to be back in time to carry on your day.

Option: fasted training means a quicker time to get out of the door; you can always eat during training (if you're cycling) or eat when you get to work (or back home).

2 Running on an empty stomach is far more enticing than bouncing your stomach around with partly digesting breakfast doing the Hokey-Cokey. Cycling and swimming are less affected but running immediately after breakfast is not favoured by many. Fasted running means you feel light on your feet, blood is not diverted from the muscles to the gut to digest food, and you move more economically as your mass is lower.

Option: eat after your run but have a warm drink, possibly caffein-ated, beforehand (likely to encourage your bowels to empty before you run).

3 You can also learn to disassociate food and training. By this, I mean the irrational need by some to always eat just before they exercise. We have inbuilt fuel reserves to take us many hours if we go slow, two hours even at a moderate pace – born out of neces-sity when we ate off the land, not via the supermarket. There is never any point in seeing how little your body can survive on; there are few events where that's promoted or logical. However, being able to train fasted is good for the soul.

Option: if you really can't go over an hour, keep sessions short, carry a carb snack for longer sessions, and always have a spare gel or two just in case you feel very light headed.

Again, in time-crunched fashion, use the evening before to prepare your equipment. Be sure any others doing the ride know that you will be going steady but there will be munching on the go. This is suitable for any sport.

Be Time-Efficient and Able to Eat as You Need

Benefits: improved time-efficiency, training the muscles' internal fat (IMTG) stores for some portion of the session, and feeding at low levels to help conserve some muscle glycogen and to teach the stomach to function to absorb carbohydrates during exercise.

Start time: this training light session could be a morning cycle to work or a run at lunch time. It's vital to start before a meal rather than eat, then suddenly decide you must train now or never.

Warm-up: again, as is the time-crunch aerobic mantra, keep the first 10–15 minutes relaxed, with the effort controlled (<70 per cent HRmax) and the terrain or resistance easy.

Main session: HR around 65–80 per cent HRmax for anything from 20–30 minutes up to 2–3 hours. Moderate effort, teaching your muscles to use the internal fats and then converting over to low carb snacks if your energy or duration means you need to consume some calories. It's not about resisting calories as you may have already done your fasted session for the week. It's just that using a modest level of food intake (when you need to), allows you to finish the session strong, without a big hunger-knock – ready to eat and continue your day.

Cool-down: take the last 5–10 minutes easy, with spin small chain ring, jog steady or reduce rowing or swimming stroke rate and effort. You would only have a small recovery drink if time suddenly gave you no other option. You must, however, eat proper food within the hour. The one time recovery drinks may be used is if the fuelling and energy levels make you blow up big time and you reach work/home in a mess. Drink 50 grams to 100 grams recovery drink mix in water as soon as possible. Then wait 10 minutes in the shower to gradually feel good again.

A Hydrate Based on Thirst

The Victorian etiquette suggestion that 'horses sweat, men perspire, and women glow' is not far wrong but must be tempered with science. Men and women both lose sweat as a way to rid the body of heat caused by muscular movement. If you didn't remove this heat it would kill you, plain and simple. So, as you sit reading this book, you're probably using about 50–80 calories per hour.

If you want to be precise, take your mass in kilograms and multiply it by 1.06 (e.g. $74 \times 1.06 = 78$ calories). So if you are a reader weighing 74 kilograms, you'll be using up 78 calories over the next hour just by sitting and reading this book. Yet start an easy jog at just 5 mph (12 minutes per mile) for an hour and you will raise energy expenditure around eightfold. Yes, eightfold for such a slow effort!

To roughly calculate energy used over an hour at 5 mph, multiply your mass by 8.7 (e.g. $74 \times 8.7 = 643$ calories). So if you weigh 74 kilograms and are using up 78 calories per hour at rest (book in hand), you would use 643 calories – or 724 per cent more calories if you jogged at an easy pace of 5 mph for one hour, instead. Do this twice as fast at 6 minutes per mile (10 mph or 16 kmh) and it would mean a whopping 1,200 calories used per hour ($74 \times 16.3 = 1,206$ calories). Many readers will clearly not be able to do this as it exceeds their ability to process fuel aerobically, but you get the point. Fast athletes just turn over the calories faster, and are economical with it.

Take Wilson Kipsang Kiprotich's 2:03:23 result in Berlin in 2013. This equates to 4:42 per mile or probably around 1,300 calories per hour for his mass. Hence YouTube footage shows the elite runners around Kiprotich passing PowerBar sports bottles between themselves (check out the video of the race at http://www.youtube.com/watch?v=pgTNGuBXR3Y 44 minutes into the footage), demonstrating that they have the modern knowledge of the need to replace fuel.

If you're fitter or get acclimatized to the training in the heat, you will sweat more effectively. This is why many serious professional and age-group athletes who qualify for the Hawaii Ironman or other hot events (such as the Ironman in Lanzarote) prepare with specific heat acclimation camps or visits to heat chambers. However, no one should try to think that being fitter means you can ignore thirst and 'try' to train your body to exercise without fluid. Again, check YouTube and the official Ironman race footage and you'll see elites drinking plenty on the bike and on the run. They can still get salt intake wrong and over- or under-hydrate – but they are drinking.

Some see sports nutrition as calories and calories as bad. Others use any excuse for a sweet tooth 'hit' using the justification of the fact they are an athlete. As with fasted exercise, which is sometimes being good, perhaps sometimes you need to ease off on the sweet stuff, too?

RIGHT NOW!

Look at your habits in typical swim, bike, run and other sessions. Do you always take a bottle of water to the pool and perhaps never drink anything on long runs? Or do you drink a sports drink during cycle training, yet rarely use it in races, even though you are over one hour on the bike and the run is yet to come? You have habits, but are they good, bad or haphazard?

In your training diary add nutrition tweaks to perfect the energy, recovery and outcome of a session. This is not a case of less nutrition means you're harder or better. Invest in good sports nutrition; it's your training and racing premium fuel.

Everything has a Maximum

You must hydrate in or after training. There will be a loss of some water which will take a few hours to restore back within the correct fluid compartments in your body. Some fluid is also stored with eaten carbohydrate when muscles increase their glycogen levels. Excessive hydration is not good for finish times, health or reducing pit-stops. It is possible, with nerves, not to listen to your body or to get your sums wrong and to over-hydrate. Many times this occurs when excessive water is consumed and very little or no significant amount of sodium (salt) is consumed. Sports drinks and gels have sodium in them to promote absorption of the water – the EFSA actually suggests carbohydrate-electrolyte drinks have approximately ½ gram to 1 gram of sodium per litre. A quick check on a PowerGel Hydro shows it has 0.3 gram per gel, so two of these an hour and you land within the EFA range of sodium, allowing additional plain water to be absorbed.

This tub of recovery mix won't do the training for you, but making your own recovery drink after a race lowers the risk of you having a service-station chocolate pig-out.

Quick Tip

Use your training diary to note hydration in sessions, reviewing it with as much fervour as you do totalling up hours or looking at race results (and who you beat). Endurance hydration does not occur by accident; it's diligent note-taking, tweaking and analysis.

Hydration before and in sessions and rehydration afterwards must be seen as a central governor to many other processes. If you dehydrate, you do not get fitter; in fact, you increase lactate levels in exercising muscle and slow the glycogen storage after training. Drinking is not weak, it is smart. You will come across some multi-sports athletes and plenty of single sport athletes as well who pride themselves on how little they use or how little they attribute nutrition to athletic performance. Here are some quotes by some endurance muppets:

- 'Leaving your gel in your cycling jersey back pocket and not using for months is a sign that you're hard and fit.'
- 'Putting a drinks bottle on poolside is a sign that you're swimming out of your league.'
- 'Riding anything less than fifty miles in training or racing with a bottle on your bike is not what real cyclists do. Not *proper* cyclists, anyway.'
- 'By not using those drinks and gels, you properly teach your body to be fitter. You don't need them if you eat a healthy diet. We never did in our day.'

To counter these luddites, look at the training diaries, interviews and race performances of top triathletes, elites or age-groupers. Elites do practise feeding at race amounts (see below) and also in some cases they do restrict fluid on moderately long sessions. However, this latter option is usually in marathoners who cannot drink and absorb enough at race pace – it's a necessity to see what they can get by on. Similarly, restricted calories may be what the super-elite Ironman athletes do to make their body eat away anything that's not required in races. They emaciate non-essential muscle and fat to get faster – going faster at all costs.

Over 100 years after the first official marathon in the 1908 London Olympics was won by Johnny Hayes (2 hours 55 minutes 18 seconds), marathoners now run in packs, passing around sports drinks bottles to aid hydration. I saw up close from the press truck, Haile Gebrselassie run a sub one-hour half marathon in Lisbon in 2008 – he was drinking at regular intervals as were others – hydration during an hour's very hot racing. In times gone by it was actually thought drinking would make you slower or even be harmful. In a conversation with Mike Gratton, 1983 London Marathon winner (2:09:43), he said he didn't drink during his race win, though with hindsight and science improving knowledge he did see that taking on nutrition in the marathon is a positive benefit – something his era was, if you pardon the pun, running ahead of.

People can run marathons and complete short to moderate distance triathlons on next to nothing apart from haphazard water consumption. But why not be faster with smart hydration? The world of triathlon has always had a good relationship with innovation and sports nutrition, but that is not to say that every contemporary triathlete is doing things right.

You must, as a time-crunched athlete, take time to use nutrition to your maximum benefit. After all, you are what you eat and drink.

Diligent Carbohydrate-Fuelling

Assuming that your session is long enough to require feeding, then you need to decide how best to achieve your session aim by using nutrition. Like buying a car, it means you have to start using petrol stations and motorway services; buying into endurance

means you have to get used to using carbohydrates for fuelling. The best athletes are not those who use the least carbs or who can recycle energy from thin air. Air and plain water have no calorific content.

Let's get a clear and concise carbohydrate feeding guide for training and racing, in place, right here, right now:

Snacking smart on rides and knowing what foods to eat the day before a race get you in the best mindset to race hard – that's the key to using diet for performance.

1 gram of carbohydrate per kilogram per hour of training

This is a rule for most sessions, though not when you're perhaps only doing 35 minutes and are well fed in the last few hours. You may also choose to do one hour fasted on water and then switch to carbs for the second hour, a tweak of the fasted session described earlier. Some even try half a gram per kilogram as a way to cut calories. However, I must make a very simple truth clear: feeding never exceeds the calories you're using – you don't get fat because you feed yourself too many carbs in training.

For example, even eating carbohydrates at a gram per kilogram, a woman weighing 58 kilograms still only consumes 232 calories per hour – about enough to carry her close to, though not quite, three miles. Let's say she runs six miles in her hour run, which equals around 540 to 660 calories, she still fails to cover 40 per cent of her energy expended. If she is aerobically cruising along calories from carbs, maybe 400 and fat use amount to 220 calories. If she is racing close to flat out to do this six miles in an hour, she could be using close to 600 calories from muscle carbohydrate (glycogen) and 60 calories or less from fat. No one will ever burn 100 per cent of an exercise session from fat – even if an instructor in a class calls it a 'fat burning session' or coach's session calls for 'max fat burning'. Carbs are, and always will be, used in training to a lesser or greater extent.

Remember: the point of your training is not to congratulate yourself on how many calories you have used; nor is it to both under-eat and under-fuel sessions. No, it is to teach your muscles to move efficiently, to channel fuel from your gut to your working muscles, to recycle lactate and trickle-feed fat into muscle. You need calories to get training to happen. Under-eat, under-fuel and be trapped by thinking sports nutrition is for other people – that's a sure way to be miserable, get ill more, get injured more, and fail to reach your potential.

You're different from Joe Public, from those who work in your office or who live on your street: you expend calories at a level that amounts to adding many thousands of extra calories per week. That's why you're always hungry, eating lots but looking fit, and why they're always eating, never hungry and looking, well, very averagely unfit.

You're an oxygen-burning machine; a calorie-combustion engine. Yet how many times have you left for a long run or ride and taken nothing, a paltry amount of water, or hoped that someone else you're going with will have enough, should you need some. Triathletes do ninety-minute swims, bike for two, three, four hours or run sixty, ninety or 120 minutes. Therefore, the planning, which can be very quickly achieved, must be to leave for sizeable sessions with fuel to do the full session well. Not just survive it.

The aim is not to arrive home having:

Hit the Wall: a sensation where your muscles gradually lose the ability to hold your normal pace – even an easy speed feels hard work; you're flat out, but crawling along. This occurs when the glycogen in the muscles drops to close to empty. You must slow down as fat reserves become the predominant fuel. However, fat can only allow very slow exercise to take place (<400 calories/hour) so it cannot take the place of the glycogen – you slow dramatically. This is also known as the 'hunger knock', 'blowing up' or 'bonked' and occurs in sessions typically longer than two hours.

Solution: eat high-carbohydrate foods (e.g. breakfast cereals, rice cakes, bananas, pasta, rice, potatoes) regularly throughout the day for at least 1–2 days before long-distance sessions and feed regularly throughout sessions that exceed 1½ hours.

Gone 'Hypo': this is short for hypoglycaemic, where the blood sugar drops, concentration is affected and vision can be disturbed. Your brain feels fuzzy and decision-making is erratic. This can occur despite good levels of muscle glycogen, so it is not hitting the wall, it's going hypo – some people call it 'bonking'. This usually happens on mid-duration sessions (60–100 minutes) when pace is erratic, possibly with sprints, and feeding on water or low carbs fails to maintain blood glucose.

Solution: feeding at the start or just before the session (e.g. energy bar, banana, dried fruit) and regularly throughout sessions (e.g. sports drink, sports energy bar or gels) when over 45 minutes, especially if the session has a high or erratic pace. This keeps blood glucose levels up to fuel the muscles and brain optimally.

Transient Hypoglycaemia – the very fact this has no slang version is probably because so few actually experience this and it may be so very subtle and so early into exercise as to be thought of as 'just the body adapting to training'. In those susceptible it usually occurs 10–30 minutes into exercise, often as a result of high blood insulin caused by eating at or around sixty minutes prior to training. For some it may be better to eat two hours before, just before starting to train, or feed in the session, not before it. It also means the food may have time to settle in the stomach, especially important in run sessions. It just depends on when the session is starting and your personal experience of feeding carbohydrates in training. I suffer from this from time to time and feed more than some others who seem to survive on thin air – it's not about how many calories you consume, it's whether you can train, race and reach your best.

Be Self-Contained – and Some

The commonplace 'rely-on-others' habit is one that I really detest. We have all got caught out, dropped food or underestimated quite how long a

session actually takes. And, my thanks to all those who over the years have fed me back to consciousness and got me home safely. However, we are all responsible for our own feeding during training sessions and should not think someone else will get us out of the mire.

Here are my top five ways to get better at carbohydrate feeding:

Have a stock of nutrition at home for when the shops are shut or you head out the door early. Keep this store up to date and well stocked.

1 **Bigger Session, Bigger Pockets:** Here training takes you up to the longest durations you're doing in each discipline. This could well end up longer than you initially planned due to enthusiasm or bad luck (e.g. a puncture or getting lost). Start out by packing 1 gram of carbs per kilogram of your weight per hour of intended training (1 gram/kilogram/hour). Plus have some emergency gels and money, especially if the final route is under someone else's control.

Good habit: prepare your nutrition and training equipment at the same time with similar attention to detail.

2 **Use All the Nooks and Crannies:** Training between home and work, in small segments of time that you sometimes manage to organize into a 26-hour day – that's nooks and crannies. With this comes the chance that it may be on the spur of the moment. So many times, nutrition is an afterthought – don't let this happen to you.

You cannot miss these sessions, or nothing can happen for days, so you have to have on-the-spur nutrition ready: crunchy bars, PowerBars or dried fruit and nuts. Put them in your desk, car glove pocket, swim bag, inside your cycle helmet, etc. – it doesn't matter where, just so long as it's handy.

This emergency fuel can be munched on just before, sometimes during and definitely after training to ensure you get something down your throat when you need it. You can survive without it, but you'll be at the mercy of confectionery, doughnuts and crisps that appear at almost every opportunity in subsequent hours.

Good habit: store snacks, emergency gels and snack money all over the place so you never get caught out

3   **Set a Timer:** If you're really bad at feeding in sessions, try setting an alarm, such as a 20-minute countdown timer, to nudge yourself into taking onboard calories and fluid. This is done by many in races, especially when, in the excitement of racing, they forget to eat or have no sense of how much time is passing by. You can't force your body to have something, but it will be better to take small amounts regularly than force the whole 750 millilitres with two gels in one go every hour. We want an amount 'per hour' to be consumed, but it needs to be spread sensibly over the hour.

Good habit: listen to your body, but if you do forget, or you train with people who fail to feed properly, an alarm may re-set the correct feeding habit.

4   **Buy Bulk and Store:** If you have the products to hand you can use them. It may be a banana with the odd PowerBar on a long ride, or an isotonic gel for a mid-distance run with a drinks belt containing water. Mix natural fruits, bars and sports nutrition products to give your taste buds some variety, but also see what works best for you. If you buy boxes of energy bars, gels or a couple of tubs of isotonic powder you can get better value. One gel brought from a shop mid-ride will be far more costly than a box from your usual bike/tri/run shop.

Good habit: have a box or at least enough for a week's worth of training stored. Ignore the emergency rations talked about earlier: that's not for the weeks ahead; that's strictly for emergencies.

5   **Be Nosy: Watch Others:** Right or wrong, watch what other people do. Maybe even ask them what they use and how much, when and so on. The more experienced and diligent the racer, the more they will have tried, tested and most likely made their fuelling habits super-effective in the day, in training sessions and for races. Never copy someone's exact regime but by all means learn from it.

Good habit: learn from others what to do (and not to do) so you can refine your feeding knowledge and application.

There is no way anyone else can exactly prescribe what you need and when. Your training time and mine and the next person's are different. However, to practise your hydration and fuelling, do think about what you take with you on typical sessions. Does it follow this rough plan of fuelling?

Less than 30 minutes	Plain water will suffice but if the session is excessively hard, has additional warm-up time or is started with you already thirsty, then a small amount of carbohydrate-electrolyte ('sports') drink will be required.
30–60 minutes	You will be sweating enough so it makes sense to drink fluid beforehand, though you may, if running, decide to drink nothing during. You could lose a litre in a one-hour session and slow recovery, or affect your appetite afterwards; try various strategies including carrying sports drink with you and sipping as your thirst dictates.
1–2 hours	The chance for blood sugar to decline, significant dehydration to occur and recovery to be slowed are the biggest issues with this common mid-distance session: it's not so long as to be feared, but is long enough to cause headaches, energy lows or immune bashing if fuelling is ignored or always goes to the default of water (penny pinching!) so hydrate based on thirst, but likely to be 400–800 millilitres per hour for most; see what makes the session outcome and recovery go the best.
Over 2 hours	This is a long session that can deplete glycogen stores in muscle and liver; plus blood glucose levels will decline if no feeding is undertaken. The 1 gram/kilogram rule (see page 143) alongside regular hydration makes this inflight refuelling, not just for long-course athletes but also sprint and Olympic-distance athletes who want to get the most from

their endurance sessions. Less fuel in does not mean the outcome of the session is better and you're somehow angelic.

Remember, the science has been done already and a good rule of thumb to get fuelling off to a good starting point is a gram per kilogram body weight per hour and drink to your thirst. For most this means 40–75 grams of carbs and around 400 to 900 millilitres per hour – the bigger and faster you are the more you're towards the top end of this scale. Your experiences gleaned from regular training nutrition intakes and the post-mortem after races allows you to hone into 'your' optimum nutrition intake.

Carbohydrate-Loading

This is probably the most known about sports nutrition strategy there is – I expect even your least active neighbour can tell you that carbohydrate-loading means eating lots of pasta 'like marathon runners do'. However, it is not just one meal, one food type or once every race rolls around. Oh, no! Carbohydrate-loading can be used in various ways to ensure that you recover better, that you get a real feel for what it does to you, and to ensure that you nip chronic fatigue in the bud.

The classic 'carbo-load' is for race week, consisting of a few nights of eating pasta – one of them maybe even the night before with a thousand other athletes in a tent. This aims to get the level of muscle carbohydrate elevated to full, thus increasing the time you can maintain a high pace. This has probably been misinterpreted by some that any race equals carbo-loading. However, it only really relates to events over ninety minutes, definitely those beyond two hours. So it is not relevant to sprint triathlon, yet is relevant for Olympic distance and upwards. This doesn't mean you deplete carbs for a sprint triathlon, then carbo-load for short events such as a sprint triathlon, a 10k run or 1,900 metres open-water swim. Excessive carbo-loading may increase your weight beyond what is ideal. Your ability to perform in the event is not optimized by super-high glycogen levels, rather the ability to deal with lactate management and pace judgement. So, why start heavy?

So that you don't always bulk-buy pasta because there's a park run 5k coming up or you have a club 10-mile time trial to ride, of course! Instead, longer races are those where you think: race week, carbo-load, plan ahead. A good schedule would be as follows:

Monday   Training tapers this week so daily duration is reduced. You may have small amounts of race pace efforts and technical drills but long sessions are stopped.

Tuesday   This and Monday can sometimes be used to back off from carbohydrates and eat fatty, protein-type foods to reduce muscle glycogen stores and make the carb-loading more responsive. It must be tested well ahead of a big event if this depletion period (Sunday evening to Wednesday morning, typically) is to be used.

Wednesday   This is the first big carbohydrate-loading day. Maintain meals at normal size even though training is tapering. Carbohydrate-rich meals are supplemented with plenty of fluid throughout the day. You can choose to drink an additional 750–1,000 ml of sports drink to maintain very high fluid uptake and ensure maximum glycogen storage.

Thursday   The process of carbo-loading continues and today/tomorrow you may want to back off as you start to feel 'heavier' and a bit bloated. After all, training is reduced from normal yet you are on a 'carbing-up mission'. For this reason you have to test to see how you react to increased mass and heaviness in the muscles.

Friday   The last big carbo-loading day and often one where minimal activity is undertaken. By now mass could be 1–2 kilograms higher as glycogen storage and rehydration maximize mass. It is not fat mass but glycogen storage that makes you heavy. Veins in arms and legs may disappear and you generally feel heavy.

Saturday   A lighter food day to reduce the stress on the body as race nerves start to kick in. Eat and drink as you feel but, as with any race build-up, try to keep to bland, usual foods this side of the race. Aim to eat evening meal early and to relax; get to bed, even if you read rather than sleep. Staying off your feet today is a good idea except for perhaps a little light exercise to loosen the bowels and get you into 'race-tomorrow' mode. As you can see carb-loading is not just for Saturday nights.

Sunday   *Race-day:* breakfast 2–3 hours before. However, the carbs are already in your muscles so eat moderately and do not pig out. Fluid intake, clearing the bowels and feeling that your nutrition intake is fine is like the build-up to any important session. If you revert to tried and tested at this stage you beat those around you who get race-day nerves and over-eat, try something untested or who go off food entirely due to over-eating the night before.

Mix in travel to a destination a few hours or several time zones away and the fact that training is declining in volume, then you see why carbo-loading is hard to get right. Practise this in a pre-season build-up event or mid-training block just to see how it feels to be fully carbohydrate-loaded. Science shows us this can increase endurance capabilities, so why miss out on the obvious, time-efficient way to fill up your tank before you've even got to the race site?

A word of caution: carbohydrate-loading is not a licence to eat lots of poor nutrient quality 'sweets', soft drinks and generally gorge big time. You're eating an athlete's diet rich in wholegrains, fruit and vegetables, for 3–5 days prior to a long event, and you're leaving the big treats (alcohol, high glycaemic treats and over-eating/excessive alcohol) until after race-day. Like a good training taper, carbohydrate-loading takes some planning and effort to keep on plan as the event approaches, despite nerves and reservations.

High-Intensity Turbocharge

The use of caffeine to improve performance is possibly the most controversial ergogenic, despite being totally legal in all formats of triathlon.

Caffeine in the form of coffee has long been connected with cycling and, as such, coffee has gradually made a link to the sport of triathlon – possibly as a result of coffee being the drink of the 'go-getters', coffee chains have grown in popularity and the connection that coffee may help training has percolated to the masses.

Meanwhile, those engaging in triathlon for the purest goals of fitness, well-being and a healthy lifestyle have in some cases seen caffeinated drinks (coffee, tea, even caffeine-laced sports drinks) as bad. Point-blank bad! Yet it is now clear that caffeine is not:

- a diuretic – it doesn't cause you to dehydrate if used before or during exercise.
- illegal – it has been dropped from the banned list. Some of the nay-sayers need to get up to speed with what WADA really sees as 'doping'.
- a slippery slope – you don't start on strong coffee before a 5k or take your PowerBar Charger pre-sprint triathlon, and then the next minute you're using EPO or anabolic steroids. Yes, it is a stimulant, but it isn't a drug.

Assuming that you want to use caffeine to go faster, the science would suggest that it can give you a few per cent faster racing. People respond differently but the majority of athletes increase their performances when using caffeine before training and competing. You can read volumes about caffeine and sports performance research; it appears to make the muscle contract more efficiently, improve neural drive to the muscle, and possibly reduce the rate at which the muscle fatigues. Hence gels, bars, drinks and pre-training load-up drinks all containing caffeine are produced by most sports nutrition manufacturers.

But, in a time-crunched world, you don't have the time to learn about calcium in the muscle and how caffeine affects it or the meta analysis of the last decade of caffeine research. So here goes:

Step 1: Calculate your optimal caffeine dose from the body mass table opposite:

Body weight			Caffeine Dose Range
(Kilograms)	(st:lb)	(lb)	(milligrams)
50	7:12	110	75–150
55	8:9	121	82–165
60	9:6	132	90–180
65	10:3	143	97.5–195
70	11:0	154	105–210
75	11:11	165	112–225
80	12:8	176	120–240
85	13:5	187	127–255
90	14:2	198	135–270
95	14:13	209	142–285
100	15:10	220	150–300

Step 2: Choose the type of caffeine you will use (*see below*) knowing what amount you need to get your desired caffeine intake (admittedly, this can be hard with unquantified sources such as instant coffee, tea, or takeaway coffee).

Step 3: Typically, take the caffeine one hour before your desired start time, however, for triathlons with open water crowded swims and varying distances here is my advice:

Sprint Triathlon (pool)   Take one hour before stated start time.

Sprint Triathlon (open water)   Take one hour before start time. Check dose to ensure no open water jitteriness or over-anxiety.

Olympic Triathlon   Take 30–60 minutes before start time. The more anxious you are as a swimmer, the closer to race time you should take it so that it has an effect once you are out of the water and on the bike.

Middle Distance (aka Ironman 70.3) As above with additional caffeine drink or gels on the bike to provide around 50 per cent of the pre-load amount, e.g. a triathlete weighing 60 kilograms could have 180 milligrams 30 to 60 minutes before and 90 milligrams (2 × 45 milligram gels) on the bike. The caffeine must be taken in the first half of the bike section to ensure it has time to take effect on the later bike/whole of the run segment.

Long Course (aka Ironman) This has to be controlled because too much caffeine could mean too hard in the swim (only 10 per cent of race time) and fatigue later in the race. Early to mid-bike is better to kick in the later section of the bike and the real challenge – the run.

For single sport events such as bike time trials, park 5k races or quality intervals sessions such as HIIT turbo session or hard and long swim set, take the caffeine as per the sprint tri race, one hour before you aim to go hard. Remember that caffeine may make you feel ready to go the second you put your kit on but you still have to warm up, control your pacing and listen to your body. It's a quick way to improve the quality of sessions. I prefer PowerBar Charger (two, three or four scoops) or Caffeinated PowerGels. Find what works for you.

The final word of warning is to use 'TurboCharge' stimulant drinks sparingly. In a time-crunched world it's easy to use caffeine to stay up longer, train when tired and turn a non-training day into a frenzy of chores way beyond your normal energy levels. Caffeine is a stimulant; use it wisely or you will run into extreme fatigue at some stage. I suggest personal clients take several weeks of abstinence immediately after the season finishes and again mid-winter to assess real fatigue.

Recovery Drinks

Now if caffeine is controversial, then recovery drinks are contentious. These recovery drink formulas are blends of carbohydrate, protein and if you're lucky (or unlucky, if you look at the price hike that results) some extra add-ons. They quickly get absorbed through the stomach into the bloodstream, spiking insulin levels, raising blood sugar and therefore pushing carbohydrate into fatigued muscle to be stored as glycogen. The protein helps both to raise the insulin level and act as a potential building block for repair – recent scientific studies suggest that endurance athletes may benefit on longer sessions by possibly using recovery drinks before or even during the session to aid protein repair.

For the time-crunched triathlete recovery drinks can take the edge off the fatigue felt at the end of a hard session or race, allowing time to dash to the shower, answer ten e-mails, help the kids with that quick bit of homework and then sit down to eat some proper food. They get glycogen in fast, aid rehydration and mean you can control your appetite and food preparation. Who actually wants a jacket potato and tuna straight after a hot three-hour ride, just after falling off the turbo trainer having done a HIIT session or when your head is still spinning from a mega swim set?

Serious sessions against the clock mean recovery nutrition has to be planned and put into practice effectively.

I was seriously excited when I read my first-ever recovery drink research paper. It was 1992, Zawadski was the author, and 112 grams of carbohydrate and 40 grams of protein was the drink in question. All written straight off the top of my head! It meant that those liquidized meals that I admitted to earlier could be replaced and rehydration, glycogen recovery and quality protein got in one quick hit!

I will not try to weigh up the pros and cons of recovery drinks over proper food. Just like you, I live on proper food, but there is a place for recovery drinks. To get the best from them, there are just a few rules to follow:

Only Use the Drinks When You Really Need Them: It's not a treat or a way to save calories on the shopping bill. Recovery drinks are for sessions where you've gone hard, long or both and finish tired and without an appetite. You knew this type of session was coming so your recovery drink should be in the fridge waiting for you when you get home.

Use the Amount that's Right for You: There appears to be no exact perfect dose, though many experts think around 20–30 grams of protein is ideal to create a significant change in the protein levels. Similarly, the carbohydrate is probably 50–100 grams to make a significant increase in glycogen storage. After all, half a scoop in water providing 40 calories is not going to help you recover, even if you 'feel' as if you've done good recovery. Experts suggest you take 1 gram/kilogram for carbohydrate intake repeated several times in the first four hours after a very stressful race or training session. Each recovery drink could amount to 300 to 600 calories depending on your body size – repeat this three times and you have 50 per cent to 75 per cent of your non-training daily requirement or the fuel used in, say, a two-hour race.

Get onto Proper Food Quickly: The flavours of recovery drinks make them moreish; there, I've said it. However, they are not real food so despite being super relevant straight after a hard session or race, plan to have real foods as soon as you can. What you will find is the fast rehydration and quick calories of the recovery drink take the edge of your ravenous appetite so you tend to eat more controlled and healthier.

Gut-Rebuilding and Over-Training Recovery

Back in the late 1990s I started writing for a body-building magazine, *MuscleMag*, thanks to the late Dave MacInerny. It was then that I read

Choose your favourite carb, protein and nutrient-dense greens to make the basis of simple but effective athlete meals.

a bit more about nutrition. It was a move that added a huge influx of nutrition, supplement and strength training knowledge to my endurance focus. A track cycling world champion once told me that 'bodybuilders know nutrition'. I agree. I was already advocating the use of whey protein, recovery drinks and creatine monohydrate. Colostrum was talked about as a great way to gain lean mass but getting a reliable source was impossible. Remember – this was before field-to-shop tracking and the internet.

To fill you in, bovine colostrum is the first milk a cow gives to her new-born calf to aid health and boost early immune strength. It contains proteins such as whey, anti-microbial factors such as immunoglobulins IgG, IgA, IgM and growth factors like Igf-1+2. Here's a summary of what I have seen published on human subjects so far concerning colostrum:

1 Improved blood buffering capacity in female rowers:
Colostrum = 60 grams per day for nine weeks
Improvement: 21 per cent higher rise in buffer capacity than control

2 Improved 5 ×10 metres sprint performance in mixed hockey group:
Colostrum = 60 grams per day for eight weeks
Improvement: significantly greater sprint improvement than when protein control group

3 Improved treadmill running in second of 2 × 30 minutes bouts:
Colostrum = 60 grams per day for eight weeks
Improvement: 2.3-fold improvement compared to control

4 Lean mass gain in resistance and aerobic training athletes:
Colostrum = 20 grams per day for eight weeks
Improvement: 1.49 kilograms lean mass gain

5 Prevention of influenza:
Colostrum = unknown amount
Improvement: 'three times more effective than vaccination to prevent 'flu

6 Improved control of resting testosterone during five days of racing:
Colostrum = 10 grams per day for eight weeks
Improvement: better heart rate variability (HRV) and testosterone balance

7 Upper respiratory tract infection in active males
Colostrum: 20 grams per day for twelve weeks
Improvement: significantly lower proportion of URTI days

On race day you can ease ahead of people who are as fit as you by using nutrition to its maximum effect. Remember: failing to fuel correctly always results in poor performance.

8 Gut permeability caused by heavy exercise:
Colostrum: 20 grams per day for fourteen days
Improvement: reduced gut permeability rise by 80 per cent

Taking 10–60 grams of colostrum per day does result in health/performance gains by athletes who were training. As part of a 'fortify yourself' for winter or a hard 'summer training block', you could fit colostrum shakes alongside echinacea tinctures, increased sleep, a wholefood fruit and vegetable diet and a low dose multi-mineral and vitamin supplement. I know more now than in 2002 when the first article went to press: more athletes admit that it's part of their plan; big teams are buying it in bulk; and the sceptics are starting to see that the benefits are multi-agency supported, not just a few one-off pieces of study.

As this book was being finished, a study from Aberystwyth on fifty-three young athletes who exercised for an average of seven hours a week gave additional support to this supplement reducing respiratory illness during winter training. With just 20 grams of colostrum consumed per day the athletes experienced less illness, in a real life but placebo-controlled study. For around £10 per week this is a useful insurance policy that may also have additional benefits to nutrient absorption, recovery time and dealing with races in the heat.

Race-Day

There is no doubt in the minds of many that nutrition really is the icing on top of the icing on the cake. It can make a difference. A *real* difference that translates to you getting to the finishing line faster, with the same hard effort that you would apply whether you had your go-go juice or not. It doesn't make fast easy, it just makes fast take less time. Too many over the top adverts, silly testimonials and 'crazes' have led many athletes to be sceptical. I'm a sceptic of the make-up industry and hair adverts in the same way. However, the scientifically undertaken, independent research on quite a few sports nutrition products shows they do work. It's not hype – it's real.

Bottom line is that you need to research and plan your race-day nutrition. I insist that clients fill out a race-day nutrition plan (see Chapter 12). This not only gets you to think about what is provided to you and therefore what you also need to take to the race (if anything), but it also means you know what key sessions should teach your gut to be able to tolerate. Train your gut in training and use this and previous races to perfect *your* race-day plan.

Remember: There is no 'one plan fits all' – you have to find your workable plan.

- There is no guarantee when you move up to Ironman that all will go to plan as it did in the last middle distance event.
- If you don't have a plan to modify to race conditions, you will under-perform.
- Even for the shortest of triathlon races, nutrition during training and prior to the event *will* affect your result.

CHAPTER EIGHT

Choosing the Right Equipment

You can buy performance or problems – you choose which.

The equipment in triathlon – let's just call it 'kit' – is part of what triathlon is all about: innovation. From aerobars to lace locks, number belts to energy gels, though they may not have been invented by triathletes, they are used innovatively to help improve speed. The 2015 bikes from Scott with nose-cone hydration systems and top tube nutrition storage integrated into the frame, such as the Plasma 5, show the process of triathlon equipment evolution is still very much happening. Sweet!

However, unless you know what the relative merits of a product really are, that the latest advert claims are really true, and these actually apply to you, you could be wasting your money or actually inserting an unwanted complication or potentially slower technology. Not all innovations in sport equal faster. A whole book could analyse the relative merits of just one of the sports and its weird and wonderful technologies.

So, what do you need to go faster? Well, it's a complicated equation:

1 Triathletes are at varying levels of kit investment to start with.
2 The potential for technology to improve performance varies across the three sports (e.g. there isn't really a 'fast' run shoe).
3 Innovation is not equal – the last decades have seen evolution mostly in enhanced bike technology, training analysis and nutrition.
4 Depending on race distance and format the relative importance of technologies varies.

So I cannot say what you need to change. I have tried many things that have turned out to be dead-ends and yet some 'prototypes' or innovative things went on to be very useful. From heart monitors (1986), aero helmets (1987), aerobars (1988), glucose polymer drinks (1989) to the now-banned glycerol (1993) and UV protective clothing (1994), which was a good idea. I like to see how kit can make the end-performance faster. Training is the most important foundation of endurance sport but technology and nutrition add to its effects, so form part of the same process. Fast wetsuits, bike and race flats don't actually do any work; they just make your toil that little bit faster.

There are certain obvious ways to ensure you go faster. This is the no-nonsense list:

1   A wetsuit that fits perfectly – and that you leave enough time to get it on correctly on race morning.
2   Goggles that fit your face, again perfectly – they must also not fog up or leak.
3   A bike that fits and that is mechanically sound, with aerobars – tweaks like tyres and rims can be significant so use the **Bike Data** form in Appendix 2 (see pages 231–2).
4   Easy entry clipless cycle shoes – that you've practised getting in and out of at speed.
5   Emergency pack on the bike, such as inner tube, CO_2 – this can save you from a DNF or just get you back quicker than if you had to push your bike.
6   Run shoes that fit and work with your mechanics – their limited shelf-life means this has more potential to hinder or harm if not regularly assessed and replaced.
7   Tri-suit that fits snugly, is comfortable for your race distance (though some long-course athletes may prefer to change) and which allows you full freedom of movement across the varied swim, bike, run activities.

You want to hit the finish line knowing for that event on that day your equipment let you show your full fitness off to the world.

I know it's a very simple checklist but it's amazing how many 'should I buy a disc wheel?' or 'my friend says so-and-so's tyres are definitely faster' I come across each week. Without knowing every detail in a potential kit upgrade scenario it's impossible to recommend a particular kit upgrade. However, if you keep a note of your equipment, at least you'll know your starting point, so make use of the **Kit Data** form in Appendix 2 (see page 230). Being your own quartermaster is a job in itself: sports nutrition stockpiles, spares for the bike, checking on shoe wear, etc. I would say veer away from trying to become the world's expert in kit across every category of swim, bike, run, technology, etc. Instead, draw on experts such as proven coaches, bike gurus, aerodynamicists and podiatrists to cut the best bang for your buck.

I spend hours talking with experts, reading research, test reports and quizzing top athletes about their methods. Even now my knowledge is evolving and it takes time, some guesswork and testing to then apply the information theory to a personal client with success. I love knowing the wattage difference a 2-millimetre increase in tyre width makes to rolling resistance and what it is worth to the 12-hour Ironman athlete. Or the optimal amount of creatine, L-Carnitine or nitrate to load an athlete's muscle to the optimum. However, don't sweat the small stuff if you can't get the basics. Instead, turn to 'Avoiding the pitfalls' (Chapter 3) or complete the following forms – **Racing Checklist**, **Race Planner**, **Race Post-Mortem** and **Race Personal Best** – to help you plan and evaluate your races (see Appendix 2).

These are some of the 'best bang for your buck' items I think (taking into account the above no-nonsense list). Do make sure that any upgrades or tweaks are worth the time, money and effort, or they end up as wasteful distractions.

> Only use what you understand and know works. Don't be an early adopter guinea pig (but also don't be a luddite).

As a triathlete, you should consider the shape of your helmet and also how easy it is to put on and take off at speed. Transition time counts.

Go Faster Hierarchy of Needs

1 Have your bike fitted to your specifications to ensure you have a perfect compromise of aerodynamics, bike-handling, comfort and delivery of power (ABCD). This is not once in a lifetime; it will need to be reassessed if you change bike, race distance, have physical limitations or degenerations that alter your physical capacity over time.

2 Tyres of a width of 25 millimetres at the correct pressure (not a default 120 psi for everyone, every scenario). For example, use Continental GP4000S II or Vittoria Corsa CX; not 21 millimetres or narrower.

3 Aero helmet that is easy to put on and take off, and is comfortable to wear.

4 Smart positioning of hydration, nutrition and spares – easy to use and reliably staying put.

5 Pre- or post-event outdoor change robe – to help you stay warm before sessions and races and dress more efficiently afterwards (e.g. DryRobe).

6 Calf guards, recovery tights and full-length socks – to help manage hard training damage, recovery and use for faster racing (e.g. CEP run tights).

7 Turbo trainer or rollers – superb warm up at races, low impact cool down after hard efforts/sessions and time-efficient/bad weather cycle training option – you can also use your race bike off-season, indoors to tweak and acclimate race position.

I could go on and on with innovations and further tweaks. In fact, athletes doing the right training, in great shape and keeping the basics easily juggled in the air do start to look at the minor details. It's amazing how far people will go to go faster (see below). Even during the writing of *Time-Crunched Triathlon* I had modest to top level athletes that I work with make changes and know of other people who changed things that they shouldn't have. For example, they would:

■ Buy an altitude tent to sleep in – they were seeking regular blood profiling to check that their diet and adaptation to the altitude regime was working.

■ Spend 3 hours getting their aerobar forearm pads and arm position optimized to reduce drag further.

■ Travel to the USA to have 1-2-1 sessions with strength and conditioning experts to help deal with lower back issues.

■ Upgrade their bike frame for the third time in as many years – plus throw in another variation in depth of carbon clincher wheels – to the three that were already owned.

■ Get their genotype assessed to see if anything has been missed or learned about how to make them faster.

■ Change their bicycle seat more times than the rest of us have had hot dinners (and even cold dinners).

Similarly, there are ways that athletes have made themselves slower. This is to get more value for money on race-day. Who actually wants to be out there longer than the minimum time? The point of racing is to have the smallest number next to your name, not the largest. Not to scare you from upgrading or ever racing again, but here's the tip of the iceberg when it comes to disasters of choosing the wrong option, namely:

■ Losing time in T2 due to cramping because they have chosen gears that are too small for the bike course hills.

■ A slower bike time because the front wheel depth and rear disk wheel are battered by high winds causing the athlete to hold the cow-horns and not the aerobars.

- Blood blisters slowing the run due to the lightweight and tight nature of run shoes.
- Slower bike due to turning back soon after starting the cycle section, re-entering T1 and putting more clothing on.
- DNF due to carrying no spares in an effort to make the bike lighter.

For the record, every one of these and more were my own mistakes, due to incorrect equipment choice. (I stopped the list before it became too painful.) Many times it is the bike section that causes hassles only because there is so much equipment that can possibly go wrong. The moral of this story is stick to what you know has a very high percentage chance of working and leave experimentation (or unknowns) to others or to testing in-training.

The crux of this chapter is to use the **Kit Data** form to keep an eye on your general equipment and the **Bike Data** form to log, monitor and tweak your bike in a methodical and effective manner. Both forms can be found within Appendix 2 (see pages 230–2). If you do decide to optimize your bike position or get filmed underwater by SwimforTri.co.uk, always get direction from experts.

You have to answer questions about your kit choices, not create analysis by paralysis. Many very smart people come into triathlon only to over-think things and therefore they never relax. A tyre is not stopping you from being your best and you probably don't have to sleep in the spare room in an altitude tent to be happy about your race results. Try to stay clear of the equipment geeks, 'know-alls' or your tri-club 'new products expert' – many of whom seem unable to actually put theory into practice yet know all the best kit to help them be a fast racer *'next* time out'. And often tell you what *you're* doing wrong in the meantime.

Over 10,000 days since my first triathlon I'm still excited about the prospect of being a competitive age-group triathlete. Some of the excitement to test my limits and to help others to do so comes from equipment tweaks that are still presenting ways to go faster – or perhaps just to offset the small decline in speed due to ageing. But, twenty-five thousand hours since I became a triathlete, it's still the hard work in training and effort on the day that can't be removed and replaced by any piece of equipment.

You have to sweat and toil to be a triathlete – just be sure to choose the right tools that help, not hinder, you.

CHAPTER NINE

Beating the Winter Blues and Greys

You may not be clinically registered as having seasonal affective disorder (SAD), however, reduced daylight length and brightness of light will suppress mood, fitness and recovery. Professional athletes and those with time and money have always seen winter training camps (or vacations) as great ways to keep training going forwards. This is not primarily because of the temperature drop that northern Europe and many other areas experience, with ice, snow and conditions far from those in iconic triathlons. Instead, it is the quality light that keeps the mood up, enhances recovery and thus reduces the winter suppression effect that the majority of amateur athletes experience.

I realize there are sceptics who want to pretend they can bash their way through winter and put the lack of quality light down as being 'all in the head'. Some professional athletes even pride themselves on sticking with the UK and battling through the winter even if, thanks to Twitter, Facebook

ATHLETE TIP

Training through the winter months can be hard to get in the hours so increase your effort by riding a heavier, cheaper road bike. In the long term this saves money rather than wastes the components on your top-end bikes. It also gives you that extra burst of speed when you return to your normal race bike come spring and summer.

Alternatives to try include wearing a weighted vest[1] or loading 1–2 water bottles with sand or nuts and bolts.[2]

ANON

and magazine interviews they seem to be out of the country a remarkable amount of times for athletes who are 'roughing it'.

There are real-life chemical processes that the sun's light triggers, and these help set your body clock for correct sleep–wake cycles, hormone release and mood regulation. This cannot be argued or just made good 'at will'. SAD is a very real clinical disorder that an estimated 500,000 people in the UK may suffer. However, at a subclinical level, few athletes experience peak performances in winter if exposed to low levels of daylight. Straight after the Olympics (or any August or September, for that matter), notice how many professional athletes disappear to Australia or similar climes that are going into summer.

> ## ATHLETE TIP
>
> When the weather is so terrible that riding your bike or running outdoors doesn't look great, have training options such as an indoor trainer, e.g. Computrainer, a standard indoor trainer or rollers.
>
> Alternatively, running on a treadmill makes for consistent running with less likelihood of injury in the UK. SCOTT NEYEDLI, *winner Ironman UK (pro) and Wales (full-time worker)*

Back in the UK amateurs start to suffer a progressive ADTS (Athlete Downward Trend Syndrome) by about October. Though much is anecdotal (much of the research combining sport and light is still rare), we are talking about a vital part of your psychology: mood. If you feel low and lethargic and a simple tool (£50–£300) improves your outlook and energy, then job done! I have measured this 'winter low-ebb', as I like to call it, and reckon on it being 5–10 per cent drop at the physiological level. This is not due to training dropping off as we see this even in very consistent athletes. However, many can lose much more than 10 per cent in their 'perceived' fitness and motivation. This is a very real issue if it makes training and competing feel harder while producing a lacklustre performance. The ADTS is as real as you want it to be, even if it is at just a 3–5 per cent level of effect. As Hamlet says: 'for there is nothing either good or bad, but thinking makes it so'.

Doctor, Light Box!

One particular example gave me an insight into how light boxes may help winter blues in athletes. A client, based in the far north of the UK, was suffering some mild depression at the time and had visited his doctor. The Doc didn't want to use medication so suggested that my client use a light box. I was unaware of the depression or the light box addition to his regime, but I started to notice that his running performance benchmarks were improving. He was better at keeping in Zone 1, also. Note that these were standard heart rate and route comparisons, so no extra effort was added; just how 'fit' his body was at that time. During a conference call one day, I commented that his running fitness was improving and that in January this was a bit of a surprise. My client then opened up about the 'depression' and the fact that he had been using the light box for a short while.

Eureka! His mood, the quality signals to his body and probably therefore his food quantity intake had all possibly made a difference. He didn't know the light-performance connection and I saw the resulting changes without knowing how it had come about. I know it's an N = 1, not controlled for my bias of light-box use, but he got better training done, in a better mood. 'Feel better, Sleep better thanks to the light box' was the comment I have recorded from him in January 2003. When many a triathlete get distracted by sexy carbon, neoprene or electronic gizmos, they could do better with smarter use of light.

I know that professional athletes can go to where the sun is, and they do. You probably can't. So bring quality light to you and your daily routine. Here are some ways how other time-crunched (or should that be 'winter-crunched'?) athletes use light to better their performances.

Many have brought a Lumie BodyClock light alarm to help them wake for early training or just to help them get out of bed on the better side. This canny clock gradually increases the light in the room,waking you up subtly from your slumber. Though this is very useful, it is best followed up by exposure to a light box during breakfast, early training (see below), or the first part of the day in the office.

Those with turbo trainers, treadmills or rowing ergometers have set the light box as close as possible to allow early sessions, or those on very low light days to considerably increase light received by their eyes. This is what several national governing bodies (e.g. British Swimming, British Cycling and British Rowing) are doing with their indoor facilities. If you are used to training very early, you'll find this useful for many months of the year.

With a shuffle around of work, getting up earlier or just using lunchtimes more effectively, suddenly my personal triathlon clients find going for a run may actually be possible. This is the easiest of the sports to change for and get outdoors into the daylight. In mid-winter your aims are: get out, start steady, switch off your work brain and enjoy the middle of the day (a very bright day is a bonus).

Those unable to train first thing but who are accustomed to waking up with breakfast, coffee and a few minutes 'coming to' have set a small light box on their breakfast bar or kitchen table. *Voilà!* You eat, drink and get a boost of light before the work day starts. Periods of light box exposure early in the day have been shown to help the release of key morning chemicals, as such, preparing the body and brain for the rigours of the day.

In workplaces and home offices, positioning a light box just to the side of PC monitors, laptops or workstations makes for easy integration. You may not be at the 20-centimetre distance usually quoted for the average SAD user's short 20-minute sessions, but you're sat there for several hours at perhaps 60–80 centimetres. I have found the Lumie Brightspark, with just a 15 × 15 centimetre footprint, is space-efficient but still effective – especially if the home office is a small set-up in the corner or in a room with little direct sunlight.

Mid-winter breaks are almost more important than summer ones – we do have longer days and sunshine (usually) in summer. The sixteen-hour days of June and July dwindle to a paltry eight hours in December. So,

The technology may make you think of *Star Wars*, but using a lightbox is a great way to fool your body and, by limiting the effect of winter SAD, prevent a drop in fitness.

to have extra days off, or half-days in mid-winter, borrow from summer allowances, to get some UK sunshine or just more daylight. This long-term strategy re-think about 'holidays' need not cost a lot as many winter breaks are discounted.

Planning time in front of a light box, outdoor exercise and exposure to whatever periods of quality light is on offer is easy. Once you have a light box you have the sun on tap!

January to late February are the hardest months. Christmas, with all those lights (no coincidence), feel-good foods (again, no coincidence) and socializing makes mid-winter slightly more bearable for some. Athletes often plan their annual training camp, long city-breaks and extra time off in the November–February window. This is to ensure that any daylight opportunities are maximized. By March (or late February, if it's a 'soft' winter) spring can be sensed, so mood upswings and aerobic fitness gains are underway.

By the way, many spouses, friends and partners have commented to athletes who have done the above that they are 'better to live with'. It's hard to argue that people tend to get 'too much daylight' in the summer so you needn't restrict light-box use in winter to short sessions only. In fact the research appearing in the last 3–5 years is just beginning to show how important quality daylight can be for health. Conversely, those on shifts or in areas of long periods of low light tend to suffer depression the most. We can get too much UV, but lights boxes do not emit UV.[3]

Light Has a Cutting Edge

In October 2013 I got invited to a special event. It was an insight into where sport is moving, as the blurb spoke about how this would 'highlight the importance or light therapy for athletes'. The event took place in Bath and it included a visit to the British Swimming Intensive Training Centre at Bath University.

So? Well, as planned, at 09.45 there was a chance to watch 'the land-sprint training in the light therapy circuit area'. Eureka! Here was yet *another* place where light was being used by top sports people to aid training, recovery and, ultimately, performance.

So, as well as British swimmers being encouraged to use Lumie light alarm clocks, they are also using light for indoor training. Sadly, I missed the event, but this idea of using light aligns with what other sporting bodies are now doing. From the special variable light levels used by Team Sky in their team bus before and after training/racing, to British Rowing equipping its athletes with light boxes/alarm clocks. (And there are some organizations doing similar things, but I can't mention them because of 'secrecy'.)

The bottom line is, the sun is our supplier of light; it's not around much in the winter in the UK (or lots of other northern latitudes), producing days that are 50 per cent shorter and often cloud covered. My nearest big cities – Bristol, at 51 degrees north, and Plymouth at 50 degrees north – are aligned with Moose Jaw in Saskatchewan, Canada. How north does that sound? Birmingham, UK, at 52 degrees north is more northerly than Calgary in Canada, the host to the 1988 Winter Olympics – think Eddy the Eagle and the Jamaican bobsled team. And both are latitudinally level with Warsaw in Poland – brrrrr! We all get short days, winter days, at these latitudes and thanks to our high incidence of cloud cover we get even less light than many other locations.

It is now even believed by some experts that the red 'ginger' pigment associated with the early tribes in the UK was as a result of thousands of years of evolution to better extract Vitamin D from the little daylight experienced in these cloudy northern regions. Ironically, people with ginger hair and freckles are perhaps better at obtaining Vitamin D, but they don't usually do too well in strong sunshine. When you don't have sunshine to boost mood and Vitamin D to assist maintaining bone density, it is advised by some experts to not only use light therapy but also to keep track of your Vitamin D status by using professional blood-profiling services (e.g. InDurance.co.uk). Though that sounds like even more time on admin and less on training, it is vital to know that the engine you're training is in good order. Training an off-balance physiology creates sub-standard results, increases the risk of injury and illness, plus it undermines the health–fitness–performance prioritization.

The bottom line is that professional athletes don't want to train with low mojo or poor health due to low light conditions of winter. They go to sunny climes, and often. You too can use the light therapy tips above. We are solar-powered. Repeat: *we are solar-powered*.

CHAPTER TEN

Coping with Injury

You will *get ill and injured. You* do *need sleep and bodywork.*

I remember the e-mail. This was never meant to happen ... It was 10 April 2013. I got it late evening. Well, 22:21 to be precise.

> Hi Joe, oh, man – the day after I got back from Club La Santa I picked up the norovirus which took me out for nine days. Then recovered from that and two weeks later picked up another virus and chest infection just two days before National Duathlon Championships. Stupidly I raced but knew immediately I wasn't right and was 3 mins slower on first 10 km than normal, although I was really fit!
>
> Was seriously ill for two weeks after the race and was in bed for a week so lesson learnt!!! Was well for a week, then had 'flu and another chest infection for a week over Easter! ... Started training again today!!! I have plenty of time to get fit again – I am *not* going to stress.

It was from Lee Piercy, a top duathlete I have coached from June 2000.

I know you, like Lee and thousands of others, don't want to get ill or injured. It stops training. It makes thinking hard and joints ache. It makes your goals seem to move further away. Your iron body, with every day of illness, is withering to that of a mere normal person. Every injury is another hurdle. Each energy-sapping illness is two steps backwards – or sideways, as I prefer to think (positively) about them.

So let's get this straight: even the best athletes on the planet get colds, injuries and low points, and you will get colds, injuries and have an accident or three. When multiple world champion Chrissie Wellington pulled out of the Hawaii Ironman the morning of the race, after leaving it to the last minute, it became clear to many (finally) that (a) elites get unwell, (b) they are able to change even the greatest of plans and (c) never say 'never' – it happens. So let's look at these things in the cold light of day and, hopefully, you're well at the time of reading this.

Illness

It's the standard infections like colds and to a much lesser extent 'flu that have the most impact on training. About 200 viruses cause the common cold and only three cause 'flu. So, the average adult catches three colds a year. Kids under six catch around six to eight (or roughly once a month in winter). Therefore, it is called the 'common cold' for a very good reason – it's common. It's not that it won't happen, even with the best diet, supplement regime, hand-washing routine and social habits (or not being social at all for that matter). A head cold can make training plans get watered down but, ultimately, the loss of 3–7 days of reduced training load is inconsequential.

Go on, read that again. You may want to jot it down and stick it inside your medicine cabinet or on that constantly re-stocked packet of 'flu remedy. When colds hit they are as much a mental challenge as a physical limiter. You don't need to fight them head on, just step around them, in a smart and calculated way. We must be very, very clear on this point, however: 'flu must be treated with respect as the high temperatures, muscle aches and severity of the debilitation are not to be underestimated. Rest is best. Pneumonia and serious illness are not our target outcome. I know you may feel fine today but when you get ill, remember what Lee Piercy said in that earlier quote. Despite months of lost training he will 'have plenty of time to get fit again – I am *not* going to stress.'[1]

Head Cold or Heart Virus?

I am not a doctor. Yet I spend every winter – yes, every winter – talking to people about their illnesses. If something stops a training week, planned event or testing session, then I have to know about it – from colds, 'flu, viruses, to infections, the lurgy, man-'flu, and everything in between. Athletes get it; normal people get it. Yet there are good and bad ways to respond to this inevitable happening.

Rambo: Do you ignore the illness and carry on training? If so, you may be seen as being 'hard', at least in your own eyes, but you'll end up making yourself very ill for a much longer time. You're now *very* time-crunched. I have seen a very, very over-motivated person put themselves on a life-support system by not listening, and then within weeks ask about 'When do I start speed work?' I terminated the coaching right there, and it taught me a lesson to watch people who never want to rest.

Smarty Pants: Do you acknowledge the lurgy but go 'touchy, touchy, feely, feely' for a few days and adapt plans, with consultation and assessment of how things make you feel? However significant these big plans or sessions is, it can all be changed for the greater good. You wrote your goals on paper (or online) not in stone, right? Don't fall into the trap that you feel good once warmed up. Endorphins and the fact that you're back training are not the real measure of how well you are: it's 1–3 hours after, in terms of energy levels to continue the rest of your life. If it knocks you down for 3–8 hours you have just done much more than your body can absorb at the moment.

Downer: Do you hit the panic button and get very down on yourself despite missing a very small amount of training? Think about it: if 300 to 600 hours a year makes you what you are on race-day, what is 6–15 hours actually going to do anyway? Most illnesses appear to hit during the October to March period. In the first three months you'll be doing modest training for skill and strength, so it's of little measurable significance for next year if you pull back because of illness. If you're ill later in winter, especially if you start to roll into late winter, events are at the most dangerous point. Nevertheless, be positive: events can be cancelled; and the faster you recover through positive action, the sooner you can be on track. Don't lose heart.

Chameleon: Does all of the above sound like you at different times depending on: (a) what you hear other people have just done in training, (b) what your rival just tweeted, and (c) what your average speed has just told you in your session? We are an ever-changing emotional animal, but try to think logically about what you can do about your health, then your fitness and how longer term these will positively help your performance.

Use your triathlon diary to note down how the slings and arrows affect how you feel.

I like the simple rule of thumb that if you have symptoms above the neck then it's probably OK to train, though respect the fact that you may be below par. Setting up a hammering four-hour ride plus a 30-minute run when getting to the end of a working day is a challenge that may be a brick too far.

Help! What Do I Do?

Viruses can affect the heart, a condition known as myocarditis, so training, especially that involving very hard exercise, can be dangerous. Other viruses just give

you a nose that could win an Olympic medal in running. It may sound common sense but if you feel 'not right', and do so for several weeks, despite adjusting your training, then it's time to get a serious check over by the doctor. Don't keep thinking about lost training time – you have to be healthy first and foremost.

Training sessions and races must have a flexible plan, or you could damage yourself – badly.

Blood Tests

Though it started in the early 1990s in a very rudimentary form, I think that blood tests are the key to keeping ahead of many illnesses and even injuries. You have some early warnings of fatigue, hormonal imbalances or nutrient deficiencies. This profiling of the internal status across many areas such as oxygen transport and immune function can show up issues before you may be aware of them. Professional services such as InDurance.co.uk are already working with triathletes to identify what's an issue, offer advice with exercise and dietary changes and follow up to see that your body comes back into the required range for best training – and maximal performance.

Having a regular blood test is something I feel will become the norm for many serious endurance athletes in the next 2–3 years. It will replace the occasional VO$_2$max test (an external output) by providing so much more clarity about what it going on across many physiological systems (the internal status). Quarterly blood testing from companies such as InDurance on everything from your red blood cells' ability to carry oxygen, to Vitamin D status will be increasingly seen as the norm. That is the future, and for those of us who are time-crunched it means even better return on investment.

As well as budgeting to have quarterly blood profiling, here are some tips to remind you to keep in good health.

Listen Up: You need to listen to your body and be your own expert. If you're listening to your body (not your training partner's goal speed or weekly target), then when things are not right you'll hear the messages. If it drags on and on, don't wait any longer: seek additional medical tests and advice. You cannot train illness out of the body. The idea that you can run a cold out of your system is up there with ducking witches and a lucky rabbit's foot.

Be Confident: Be easy on yourself so that your long-term ability is not affected by a short-term illness. It's not the person who beats the most colds who becomes the fittest. Every year a few of my clients lose a lot of time through illness, yet they still manage to get back to their peak, if somewhat later in the season than they would have liked. But they do get back. Cold and bugs just affect your current health and fitness to perform – not your long-term genetic ability. As Ludovica Bruno, age-group winner in many races, e-mailed me at the end of a season:

'Well done to you! You rescued me from two months' illness and prepared me for an Ironman and the World Championships in London. I am extremely grateful.'

Backdate: Right now look at last winter's training diary and the year before that. Yes, in there are periods of illness but you got through them, and still achieved much the following year. Pay attention to any pre-warnings that suggest you're teetering on being ill. It could be feeling the cold more, having a 'buzzy' head, everyone else going AWOL, a drop or increase in sugar cravings, or any one of many more niggly things. Spot these and you can be pre-warned (but don't go all hypochondriac on me, either).

Don't Go Quiet: I can tell when some people get ill: they go quiet; they get amnesia and stop filling out their diary. Instead of writing how they feel, instead of watching the 'score out of ten' improve from 3 to 6, instead of being 'real' and noting that they do get ill, they selectively drop out and mope. They have just learned zilch from the event. So be proactive with how you tweaked sessions, used medication, missed work or whatever goes on, and see this as part of the cycle. No one is 100 per cent fit and well all year round – get that clear and you can deal with illness, injury, major life events and just about anything.

Fly Then Die

This is not quite as dramatic as it sounds, but still it plays out for many at one time or other. During perhaps a standard training session or a race you get a quite surprisingly good performance. An almost 'best that I could possibly feel' type of performance. You 'fly'. This happens often for a training session because there are so many of these in comparison with actual races.

However – and lucky for you – sometimes this 'fly', then 'die' scenario unfolds during a race: you go very well, as good as you could have expected, then the illness hits within hours or, at the most, the next day. One day later and the illness would have crushed your race. This is not the race making you ill, but you racing when just about to get ill – in effect, racing as your body is getting ready to fight all those invading bugs.

This isn't something that can be manipulated. If only we could catch a bug that makes us go well in our race, then make us ill the day after. I would advise, though, that you always look out for something that feels too good to be true: not because I don't want you to go well, but the more you use it up, the greater you're digging yourself into a hole. If the session was never meant to be a test to get a personal best for your loop, why turn it into one just because you 'feel good'? Training is planning what you do, not reacting to when you might feel good enough to have a go at a personal best.

Injuries: Tripped or Tripped Yourself

There are accidental events in life. Some are not in your control, others are caused by you being, well, out of control. Then there are repetitive

If you train by doing short bikes before your run sessions, this may ease your muscles into being warm and ready for the rigours of running. It's certainly race relevant.

actions that worsen the organism. Even downright self-inflicted damage. Injuries are something that some seem to dodge and duck out of – others have a magnetic affinity to them. If you always term them in the same broad brushstroke of 'injury', it can miss the point: was it in your ability to lessen or not? How can you increase the chances of this *not* happening again?

RIGHT NOW!

Fill in the **Body Database** form in Appendix 2 (see page 233). This I feel is one of the best tools for the time-crunched athlete. Use it to make note of your past and present injuries, surgery, niggles and limitation, and when they happened. From one leg being 8 centimetres shorter, knee surgery (twice), heart bypass and elbow dislocated, to hamstring sore, wrist arthritis niggling, calf cramping in sleep and vastus lateralis (left) tight. It gives you an idea of what you're dealing with, from the big and scary to the most recent niggles. This can help pinpoint what bodywork you get to how you set up your bike or vary your shoe size.

I can't wrap you up in cotton wool; nor do I have the answers to 'Why did I fall off or trip over?' or 'Was it that excessive run that injured my calf?' However, I've found that using the Body Database form (see page 233) can help athletes like you to keep a track of anything that is significant. It's not meant to be a war wounds sheet to compare on those cold, dark nights, nor is it to give you an excuse for your lack of performance. Instead, see it as a way to quickly get to what is most likely to be the reason behind certain issues. You can't remember every injury. In fact, I would advise you to forget every race result or shoe brand that has ever worked for you, and instead try to remember your injuries. Use the Body Database form and refer to it regularly. I've found that the body map works out to be like clues in an episode of *Poirot*, slowly drawing you towards a (mostly) correct conclusion. Keep it updated and you'll know your enemy – the over-use or degeneration of the human body. Endurance sport is, after all, as much about keeping it going over time as it is racing each year against the clock.

Make a note of any experts who helped with injury rehab, surgery or specific strengthening exercises – these should be on the 'Experts' section of your Vital Information form (see Appendix 2, pages 245–6). You used these experts once before, so you may need to use them again in the future. I've found that it often takes me several experts to identify and cure a problem so you should compile your expert database by keeping track of who did what and when. That way, when the next person working on you asks 'What's the story about this injury, then?', you can give them the details. Think of your Body Database form (page 233) and Vital Information forms (page 243–7) like a biological passport for injuries.

I can't tell the speedy types to ease up on technical parts of a race or the keen to always do the training when it's relevant. I can't tell you the best running shoe or why you sometimes get a shoulder impingement. That's the area of another expert. But I can guide you to becoming an expert on you, keeping good records and realizing it's a mug's game to just train as much as you think others might be doing or ignoring your body when it sends you massive neon warning signals to change course. Injuries can stop your triathlon career – always remember that.

I can tell and assure you that lots of people make mistakes that they wished they could have avoided, if at all possible. You can still learn by your mistakes; it's just you can learn plenty 'without' mistakes.

Read that again. You don't *need* to stretch something to the point of breaking to allow it to grow and thrive. I guess this is borne out by research that shows 90 per cent of HRmax intervals are more effective than going several per cent harder. *Nurture, don't knacker.*

Working hard gets results but only if your body adapts to the stress and is not broken by it. Be careful with your intervals as well as how you run on hard surfaces.

I am guessing – no, I'm vehemently arguing – that it's also a faster way to progress because mistakes not uncommonly come with a 'three-steps back' clause for the one step you (eventually) make forward. If you're short on time or a bit heavier, that's fine: it's OK.

However, if you're injured or need surgery, much more time and potential problems exist for you, now and in the future. The human spirit to overcome adversity is an incredible thing but why be a hero of injuries when you could be talking about your last event, not your current woes?

This time-crunch chapter puts other things ahead of training. It's a footnote chapter for those looking for the kit pages and where I say 'Yes, you need a disc wheel'. This message is important and has a big impact on your performance, so bear with me. I know it's heresy to think of putting something in place of a training session – you're already time-limited, after all. However, there is a very high – no, a definite likelihood – that training (and life) will cause muscle or joint issues and illness. Yet many issues can be managed or eliminated by seeking and regularly using professional experts – what I term 'body workers' – from a masseuse to a physio, a chiropractor to a Bowen therapist. These people are not just there to pick up the pieces when you build up issues to breaking-point, but are, in fact, there to be invested in, long term.

If your training aim is to be consistent and to gain strength, skill, efficiency and endurance, a healthy body is the foundation. No one actually runs their best with a hamstring niggle, bikes really well with lower back pain, or can swim at the top of their game with a shoulder injury. Use the body map (see appendices) to help you monitor your niggles and learn about your body.

A bike-fitter may spot you have a leg-length discrepancy, an ex-pro notice that your hamstring is tight on the left when you run hard – people will give you insights into the physiology, good and bad, that you have to work with. Noting issues and insights on the body map makes this more like a list of MOT faults and, importantly, how they were rectified.

Know your bike set-up, even at the simplest level, so you're quickly able to correct a seat post that drops down.

No doubt there are great new wheels, wetsuits and the like to tempt your cash elsewhere, but I go on and on to clients to seek the best body-workers they can find and use them regularly. Some ignore good advice but they are the ones whose performances are not consistent and who regularly have problems with their body.

I won't go into the in-depth science of stretching, foam rollers and other self-help at length, but rather advise a few pointers. Without you right in front of me, this will make for a better way to integrate these elements of body management:

1 **Stretching/Foam Rollers:** Do so after your sessions. Stretch for 30 seconds before repeating, and concentrate on known areas of tight-ness, not areas where you're close to circus-contortionist ability. Never use instead of an aerobic warm-up.

2 **Experts:** You need to be consistent and still use experts even if you've resolved the most recent niggle or scare. This is good use of time on a recovery day. Don't try to self-heal everything, or be an expert in yet 'another' field.

3 **Look at Lifestyle Biomechanics:** You train far less than the movements and strains that work puts on you. Bad driving posture, lifting two tonnes of cement, flying in cramped seating, or even changing to stiff-heeled shoes (or higher heels) can all add more than training ever does to the injury or niggle list.

Relaxation is the key to recovery from training. You may be time-crunched, but you must never think that relaxation is a waste of time.

It's a Ying–Yang approach, where training (and life itself) produces issues that must be managed. This is vital for muscle recovery, joint mobility and to offset the damage that inevitably comes with sports (and that damned work that gets in the way of training). Keeping at this game for a long time requires mindful body work. Oh, that and Vitamin Z ... (see page 191).

ATHLETE TIP

If you only have an hour to train at lunch, ensure that ten minutes of it is allocated to stretching post-exercise. This will help stave off injuries, especially as you get older.

LEE PIERCY, *Powerman Arizona winner 2015, World Age Group Duathlon Champion 2014*

ATHLETE TIP

Bring the mini grid foam roller on every flight you take and wear compression tights on flights.

LEE PIERCY, *Powerman Arizona winner 2015, World Age Group Duathlon Champion 2014*

ATHLETE TIP

Turn into a yogi on long-haul flights. How often do travellers complain of back trouble post-flight? Sitting uncomfortably for many hours on those airline seats is a nightmare for the back so find a space (in the galley near the toilets) to do some stretching every couple of hours – it makes a world of difference to how you feel post-flight.

LEE PIERCY, *Powerman Arizona winner 2015, World Age Group Duathlon Champion 2014*

Bodywork is Always Worth a Try

'At the age of forty-two, after many years of karate and running, I decided a new approach was needed and took up triathlon as a new way of keeping fit and focused in a competitive environment.

So in 1998 I entered my first triathlon at Taunton Deane sprint. I was hooked. Longer distances soon became my focus and (with coach Joe Beer's help), I progressed to Olympic distance and in 2001 the first Half Ironman UK (HIMUK). In 2002 it was the Longest Day (Ironman distance) and the second HIMUK: this was to date my best year for results.

At the end of 2002 I began to suffer with my back and in 2003 this became difficult to deal with. Degeneration of the L4/L5 joint was the diagnosis, an epidural injection was the way forward and I was advised to stop all activity .... Disaster!!! I ceased all sport, but the pain was still there and, if anything, was getting worse.

A spinal operation was suggested (with associated risks); a different approach was needed. At a chance meeting with a chiropractor over a business breakfast, he suggested that he could solve most back problems. Although some cost was involved I was happy to take the risk of this new approach if, firstly, I could get relief and, secondly, return to some sort of activity.

Straight from the first treatment the improvement was frankly amazing, and not only was the improvement by reduction of the pain but gradually I felt I could begin light duties, and even started running. Although frequent chiropractic adjustments were needed to keep the pain at bay, I needed a target. The 2005 Ironman UK was selected and, ultimately, completed. During the intervening years I have seen two other chiropractors and between each have had a fair 'dormant' period during which the original level of pain returned. My current chiropractor takes a holistic approach to her craft and looks and corrects the whole structure and the way it can affect the spine. Monthly visits keeps things aligned so I can remain active.

I am convinced that without chiropractic help I couldn't compete in triathlon, entering 2–3 long distance events a year plus various shorter distances and all the associated training. Whether or not you have a problem it's worth a try.'[2]

DAVE AMBLER, *twelve-times Ironman; coached by Joe Beer since 2000*

Keeping it All in Perspective

In order to deal with the inevitable crises that will come your way eventually, I would like to paint a picture, less about time efficiency, and more about perspective. It makes the tough seem a bit easier; makes the often tiny issues seem, well, irrelevant. Over to triathlete Chris Goodfellow:

Crash!

'In May 2010 I had an major bike crash while racing Ironman Lanzarote. It was a serious one. I had a brain haemorrhage, fractured vertebrae and severe memory loss – immediately after the crash I thought it was 1984 and while being airlifted was very worried about how they were going to fit the Star Ship Enterprise into the plane. I don't even like *Star Trek*! The events that followed still spin vividly around in my mind today, almost four years on ....

The aftermath of the crash? I really don't remember much. Everything is pretty blurred, like watching a film in fast-forward. It all just rushes by, but your mind does take in a few screenshots here and there. For me a few 'screenshots' are imprinted on my memory:

- Looking at myself in the mirror for the first time at the hospital – I looked like a monster!
- Being given some *cool* new clothes – I had nothing to wear (I still wear those clothes with pride to this day)
- The flight home – everybody was just staring at me (Did I look *that* bad? Really!?!?)
- Staying at my parents' house and sleeping *all* the time.

It's important for me to explain my state of mind at this point and this is really hard to put into words. As far as I was concerned I was 100 per cent OK. Sure, I had a few (*a lot*) of cuts all over my body, but they were healing really fast. OK, I was sleeping most of the time. But none of this really registered in my mind as an issue. When I was awake, my mind felt great, laser-focused on the next race (ITU world long course championships) in two or three weeks. The trouble was, that didn't last long and I was soon back asleep. It is hard for me to explain just how focused I was on the next race. My last memory was of running out into the waters and starting the swim in Ironman Lanzarote, then … nothing ….

It was like my mind was still in *full on* race mode. I get this type of tunnel vision where my mind blanks out everything outside the race. That is the only way I can really describe my state of mind after the crash. *Totally* focused on the next race. Everything else just became, well … background noise. I can't say I'm proud of this. I would've loved to say that, at the time, I was thankful of being alive and so very appreciative to all my friends and family for their support. Looking back at the event now, I can't believe just how amazing everyone was – a testament to how truly kind people can really be. But at the time … It was *all* about 'the next race'.

The first event that I can remember fully (or at least I thought I did) was the appointment with the GP. I thought I was doing great and that the appointment was more of a formality to confirm this. I remember chatting to the doc about what had happened and towards the end of the assessment I asked more as a formality 'so when do you think I will be able to start training again?' The Worlds were in 2–3 weeks, I had been lying in a bed for more than two weeks so I wanted to get a few sessions in beforehand. His response 'maybe *gentle* exercise in *six months* … !!!!!!! It's hard to put into words what I felt at that moment. I think the best word to describe it is PURE ANGER and that 'anger' only intensified my single-minded *race focus*.

The severity of the damage to my brain I think is only really obvious to me now, looking back on things, some four years later. Like I said, at the time I felt 100 per cent normal, but talking to Carli (my then girlfriend – now my wife) or 'Doris' (my Mum; this is her nickname – a long story …) about how I was after the crash, I was quite clearly *not* OK. I was short, very aggressive in my nature and generally just not me at all. It's strange to chat to them about events like that doctor's appointment. My memory of what was said and how I was is so far out of sync with what actually happened and was said, it's just not true. That is why writing this is so hard. My memory of events and what happened seems to be a little 'out of shape'.

So, back to that doctor's appointment – and my response. I just did exactly what I thought was the logical thing to do having been forced to cancel all the season's races. I entered new races: Challenge Barcelona in October and Ironman Cozumel in December. Then I got back on my bike!

While writing this, I went back to look at my training diary to see how long after the crash it was that I got back on the bike. I figured it must have been 3–4 weeks or something. It was actually fourteen days! Looking back at it now, that seems totally crazy.

I guess it's just my nature. When I get 'pushed', I push back, and this was my way of 'pushing back'. Not surprisingly, the first time back on the turbo was not good. It was so bad, in fact, that I don't think I've ever spoken about it to anybody. My brain immediately started to feel 'funny', then everything went blurry, the back of my head started to hurt and I had to get off. I had only lasted four or five minutes, if that. Not the 'push back' I had intended! I have no idea why, but at the time I wasn't too worried about it. I just thought to myself – OK, I just need a few more days for my brain to heal up, then I will give this another go. And that is exactly what I did. The next time I managed 26 minutes at 200 W (40 per cent of pre-crash peak power) with no issues! The day after, I did 40 minutes at 200 W. My 'push' was getting stronger and things just went on from there ....

To me, at the time, those races I had just entered (Challenge Barcelona and Ironman Cozumel) were my lifeline, a light at the end of a very long, dark tunnel. I was holding onto that thought of racing again, with everything I had. Every day, I would do a little bit more than I had the day before and slowly but surely, it felt like I was beginning to climb out of that tunnel. With every session I did, I felt more awake, more alive and a little bit more like me. That's the best way I can describe it.

As the summer went on I got back into full training and my body was doing great. I was flying in training. But that red mist that surrounded my mind after the crash remained. I just couldn't shake it loose. Ironically, this red mist cleared in a single moment: at the start of Challenge Barcelona. At the time I wrote a blog 'What doesn't kill you makes you stronger' and I thought I would let my writing from 2010 do the talking:

Standing at the start of the Challenge Barcelona (Ironman distance triathlon race) I took a step back from it all and watched the sun rise. It was a pretty emotional moment for me. Four months ago I was in a hospital bed on Gran Canaria, having suffered a brain haemorrhage and fractured verte- brae from a bike crash while racing Ironman Lanzarote. That now seems like another lifetime away, or a bad dream. In the months after the crash my mind seemed to be stuck in race mode and was unable to let go. I have been totally focused on racing again with little room for much else. The reality of this meant that I have been my own worst enemy, and was forget- ting what really mattered, enjoying every second of living and the people around me.

Standing at the start of it all seemed to make sense. Sure, I was going to give absolutely everything I had in the race today, but the red mist that had been clouding my mind for the last four months was finally lifting. I was just appreciating the view and chatting to the people around me ... Running down the finish chute this time was a blur of emotion. This was so much more to me than just finishing another Ironman. It was putting to rest the crash in Lanzarote and all the shit that followed. I was close to tears. I can't really explain what this meant to me. I had no idea how I had done in the race, and if I am truly honest I don't think it really mattered.

One more thing was left on the agenda for the year – Ironman Cozumel. My performance in Barcelona had been slightly slower than I had hoped for and aimed for (9 hour 26 minutes). I was better than that, and I was determined to prove it. I never managed to 'prove it' in Mexico – that had to wait until Challenge Copenhagen 2012, (8 hour 47 minutes), but I did come away with a slot to the World Ironman Championship in Kona, Hawaii. *The* Ironman.

Every time I think back to 2010, it puts a smile on my face; it really does. Even as I am writing this, the memory of it all just makes me smile.'[3]

CHRIS GOODFELLOW, *triathlete, coached by Joe Beer from October 2009*

Chris Goodfellow came back from adversity to produce some of his best-ever races. He continues to race and train, and is a true family man who balances triathlon in a time-crunched scenario – just like you.

Traffic Lights are One Cure, Too Many Ills

In your diary, indicating by colouring in a cell or writing across the day/date, gauge how you feel by using a traffic light system to summarize how things are going. It's meant to be a varying blend of colours in which you can see trends and reasons for why certain things unfold. It's not that you won't have adversity, it's how you deal with adversity that counts. And 'red splodges', as I like to call them, are either small, occasional hiccups or major head-scratching forehead furrow-makers. 'Red splodges' can keep you awake. They mean digging deep for ways to keep positive, trying new methods or just accepting the best-laid plans always have deviations when they meet reality.

So here are your traffic light definitions:

Green: you're moving along nicely in expected fitness, health and performance terms. That day, that session, that week was a good solid move forwards. These are sometimes a yellow but a few details make it seem like progress was made. Remember you're only trying to get 2–5 per cent better, so every hour, every day, is a tiny increment of gain. Much is good in your world, and if it's not, then don't just score the training and miss the pending divorce, downsize or death in the family.

Training is a way to deal with adversity and to put yourself to the test in events that whet your appetite.

Yellow: OK, but just that; no signs of a step forwards (yet, not backwards, either). Plenty of days are like this; there cannot be movement forwards all the time. It may be you just failed to measure gain, but if there were no losses these are fine. If you only give green or red you may be missing the point that yellow is OK to give. It's just shows you're either on a plateau, still making internal and mental positives moves forward – but it's not yet obvious.

Red: something has hit the proverbial fan quite hard (or hard enough in your world and perspective) to be irritating. It could be work messed up your training for two days. You got a migraine. A race ended up with a 'did not finish' (DNF). You're ill for the fifth time this winter. This stuff happens and if you don't acknowledge these things, then you're too mentally fragile to admit that you have bad sessions, bad days, bad weeks. It happens: you just have to acknowledge it, then see what you

Yes, I know the picture shows my right fingers spread just before entry into the water. To save drag, the fingers need to be closer (that's half a per cent just found).

Simple self-massage and other devices like The Stick and foam rollers can help you to keep on top of muscle damage and tightness.

On those days when things feel just amazing and you raise the bar on what you thought you could do – well, welcome to Gold!

A diary is an essential training tool for the time-crunched athlete.

can do to dust yourself off and get back to better colours in the traffic light ....

Gold: and no, this is not what you were expecting after the red, was it? This is a stupendous session, race outcome or even a technology aid added to your arsenal that raises the level you can attain. It puts your performance above what you could imagine; you're on track for your very best. These can even happen the day after a red day, perhaps when time made you down and off-plan, then you leap forward out of the blue. This is a 'green' moment but with added vigour, surprise and opens up new possibilities as to what you might be able to do. Perhaps even reassess future goals? You don't force these to happen; they just come about through the green, yellow and even red days that you have accumulated, learned from and made smart actions because of.

As a time-crunched athlete, you must use time and information to your most efficient outcome possibilities. A diary is your way to plan, review and learn the best ways to be fitter, go faster and be technically superior. I would suggest a monthly review of what you've done and what you're about to do.

If you have a diary right now, go back six months and see the training, tribulations and teachings that it shows you. From just a single glance back to a few weeks' training you can get a boost of motivation, a reminder of things not to ignore, and a few chuckles at what you did. This is your book and it goes hand in hand with your diary. There's one thing many people could really do with monitoring in their diary ....

Vitamin Z Dosage

Studies into athletes' sleeping patterns shows the better the athlete, the more they protect their sleep, usually sleeping in the 9–11 hour range. Per week this mean over 60 hours' sleep; in some, over 70 hours. So professional athletes are lazy, right? They take more sleep, naps and down-time in the day. Read this BBC Sport report to see how sleep research is now shaping football: http://bbc.in/1byzMPt.

Firstly, that's what an athlete's 'working' day is for: training or recovery. Secondly, if you want muscles to adapt to training, then the best antidote *is* sleep. It's the down-time, the re-set button, the chance to grow. I suggest as well as body work, you take time to keep a track of your sleep hours. Not if everything is OK; rather, if you're not recovering or always putting work first, the kids (or the cat) are always waking you up. If sleep is an issue, get it sorted and if possible aim for over 50 hours per week.

To get a relaxing sleep, try to ensure that your bedroom is a calm environment, without a TV blaring or everything untidy. One athlete made so much difference to their recovery by just clearing out the exercise bike (unused) and a tonne of clutter from their bedroom. Wake-up lights (e.g. Lumie) can bring you nicely alert in the morning rather than making you jump when an alarm sounds – they also gradually dim in the evening to bring on a relaxing dusk-like scenario. If it's good enough for the likes of British Swimming and other sporting bodies, it's probably worth trying for your sleep, too.

- Track your sleep totals to see if you really do need to focus on a simple way to get more energy and absorption of training
- Look at your illness and motivation lows – do these correspond with low sleep periods?
- Think about naps, forty-winks while travelling and power naps – is it possible for you to get sneaky recovery and be full of beans more often?
- Sleep is a simple way for even the most time-crunched to get ahead; not by trying to get less, but by helping them to perform at their best at work, at home and in triathlons. Sleep – you need it!

CHAPTER ELEVEN

Getting the Lifestyle Balance Right for You

Races give us a 'feelgood' factor. They can make us feel younger again. They can show that we can overcome hurdles and achieve much. However, whereas for a very few select athletes, races actually pay the bills, *you* pay to race, *you* have to buy your equipment and the time *you* spend on training is often about *you*. Let's be honest about that.

To be good at sport requires that you're selfish to some degree. Those on the quest for Ironman distance events, qualifying for the hallowed Kona event or to rack up ten, twenty or thirty of the things, need to be selfish. However, the key is learning if, when and for how long you can focus on *you*. I realize some readers make a lot of their life choices to allow training to be optimized and racing to be a very high priority. The spiral of racing success and training to reach your best is enticing. However, it never just keeps building. Every athlete needs down-time, needs to know when to back off, when they need to invest in the rest of their life. In the era of work–life balance being much talked of, you as an athlete must think about triathlon–life balance.

This requires thinking, planning and doing things that are not about training but about the bigger picture beyond the triathlon bubble that can engulf anyone who gets 'hooked'.

Those that knew me as the twenty-something student, ex-runner turned triathlete would have laughed at that time had I mentioned the word 'balance'. Now a husband and father of three, with a packed

Triathlon is a way to find out about yourself and to enjoy many great natural areas to train and race in. Unless you are pro, it's not your career or epitaph.

business schedule, I have many other factors to think about. It's not just about my training. Over those two and a bit decades I have coached clients to be balanced, learned balance from many great friends in the sport, and have matured in my outlook. Honest, I am still competitive, love to race the next person in events but realize that balance is key. Excess is a bad platform from which to help others, and be the best dad, husband and friend. I'm still learning.

Learning

As a coach you learn from research and smart-guessing an athlete's next block of training, maybe where things could be better next time around. Two or more brains are engaged in an athlete–coach relationship and this, when used with full clarity of perspective, makes for an amazing learning machine. One great example for me of this two-way process when working with a smart cookie is my client Mark Rickinson. He has epitomized the process of keeping things in balance, despite the ease with which obsession and selfishness could have badly affected his work, family and personal growth. Over to Mark ...

Balancing Tri and Life

'My wife would cry with laughter if she knew that anyone was asking me for advice on how to have a balanced approach to triathlon! But it's something that I've tried to work on over the years. What I've come to understand is that the best way for me to improve is to be consistent, and the best way for me to be consistent is to be balanced. And being balanced has been about finding ways to do the following:

Face up to the risk: Triathlon is great for lots of reasons, but it's important to face up to the fact that it is (or can easily be) a selfish sport. When I first heard that said by an experienced triathlete I immediately wanted to challenge or dismiss it. Over time, though, I've come to see that, if left unchecked, the focus on my training, my sleep, my nutrition, my kit, my races, etc, can create big problems for other areas of life. So facing up to this risk is key.

Prioritize balance: Like most triathletes, I am well into goal-setting. In more recent years, though, I've started to include 'balance' goals alongside performance targets. So in 2013 I wanted not only 'To get top 5 in age group at New Forest and Costwold113', but also 'To keep tri training/racing in harmony with Mary and the boys'. I've found making this type of statement at the start of the year helpful as a reminder that race results cannot be at the expense of family harmony.

Choose your mentors: If you want to get better at taking a balanced approach, then you need people around you who will support that way of being. I've been lucky to have found a coach (Joe Beer), an osteopath (Andy Jackson in Reading) and a few blogs (e.g. Gordo Byrn's posts on Endurance Corner) and books that time and again have helped me to keep triathlon in perspective.

Schedule your training and racing carefully: Keeping triathlon in balance with other aspects of life is a hell of a lot easier if you make smart choices about training and racing. Smart choices for me have meant: taking Saturday as a rest day; using lunchtimes and commutes as key training slots; doing a lot of my training solo; always favouring local events as much as possible; and (sounds silly but …) knowing how to get changed quickly.

Know when to focus: A balanced approach doesn't have to be about mediocrity. Being competitive as an age-grouper requires focus, effort, attention to detail, perseverance and dedication. There are key sessions that need to get done and getting them done can require some selfishness. But these should be the exception rather than the norm. So know when you really need to focus and don't waste time, effort and brownie points on things that aren't critical.

Know when to let go: To enable improvement over the long term, you've got to find ways to kick back and let go of everything connected with swim/bike/run. A rest day when you don't talk about tri at all, a Christmas holiday where you just run for fun with your kids, a mid-season break where you indulge and have fun, a post-season period where you put energy into other areas of life, and now and then a season off to focus on improving in a single sport or doing something totally different.

Know how to train without training: It sounds strange, but there's a lot you can do to improve your race performance that is not about training. Eating well, sleeping well, sorting kit, finalizing your race plan, booking accommodation, doing positive visualization are all examples I have found work well. Getting stuck into doing these kinds of things has really helped me to deal with those situations where child-care plans go pear-shaped, work goes crazy, or you're just too knackered to train.

Learn from disasters: However hard you try there will always be times where it all goes disastrously wrong. I never again want to live through trying to complete peak Ironman-build training during a three-week family summer holiday! I thought a late season local iron-distance race would be a good option as there would be no travel involved and I could build up slowly over the summer. I just hadn't realized how critical August would be for training, or what a nightmare it would be trying to do it while on holiday. Lesson learned the hard way!'
MARK RICKINSON, *triathlete, coached while living in UK and Australia, JBST athlete 2006–15,*

The Much Bigger Picture

By 'the bigger picture', I don't mean just pack it in for six months and build that extension you've always been talking about. There is no model, no novel hand-held device or a simple online questionnaire to complete.

However, keeping the much larger viewpoint, knowing that triathlon is a part of life, not the only thing in life, means you can constantly adjust your actions to the conditions that prevail around you. In the era of being time-efficient, thinking about end-goals and achievements. It may be hard to think about the perspectives and ideas of others. Yet doing so is *vital*.

Take the following as a litmus test to keep you on an even keel:

1 **Ask the other half:** Yes, he or she probably knows when you're over-doing it far sooner than you do. They see your mood swings, see when things get sidelined to allow extra training to take place, and know when you have had a bad race-day. Use their opinion to good effect and you will learn faster *and* have a smoother relationship.

2 **Identify the offenders:** If you can see other athletes who clearly know how to be selfish, unbalanced and obstinate, then it's a clear reminder of what *not* to try to emulate. The moment people start to talk about you in terms of your excesses and single-mindedness it's time to seek help from all those around you. It's so easy to justify excess in others, but to rationalize what *we* do as necessary for our goals. You don't need to give up endurance sport, but you must allow it to be in harmony with your whole life.

3 **Think efficient, not more:** It's very easy to think that extra hours equals extra fitness, better races and your name appearing in lights (or less in the dark). In reality, a single training session or even great over-load week for that matter does not actually massively change your future performances. It's about consistently trying to nudge your genes and work on your weaknesses. However, if all around you are on the defensive because your training is taking up too much time, you can't keep it going anyway without massive disruption. Training to a divorce or P60 has been done. Work out the time you can invest, the sessions that work best, and then be happy to switch off and get on with the rest of life.

Work to ensure that training and racing don't keep out the significant people in your life before your next personal best training session or trip away.

4   **Watch the non-training faff**: Some triathletes say they don't train too much but at every opportunity they are *non*-training. For instance, reading another training article on their laptop while their friend is sat opposite them chatting away with a coffee; they over-analyse the last session instead of admiring the view; they talk about races to people who care little but put on a brave and interested face. Does this sound familiar?

Watch this creep of tri into every spare minute you have. You must switch off; do nothing to do with training or racing; be happy with the rest of your psyche. The goal is balance, not excess, I happily remind myself visually from time to time with a Ying–Yang tattoo I have on my hip (luckily, I was in a cool San Francisco parlour when getting the 'a tattoo would be cool' thought, and had not just finished a race).

REDUCE STRESS, MAXIMIZE CONSISTENCY, INCREASE FUN

The key aspects I took from [Joe Beer's] … advice, which I believe are important to any age-grouper with young families and busy lives are:

1   **Family balance:** this is key to consistent training and longevity.
2   **Time management:** your training plan should focus on how it best fits into your life and not focus on how many hours or miles you feel are needed to achieve a goal.
3   **Communication:** work with your better half on how best to plan your week so they can help you train smart and reduce the impact on family or partners, which should then reduce stress to yourself and make sure that everybody involved is on the same page.
4   **Key sessions:** work out your key three sessions per week and highlight them in your training log. Try to hit these each week so even if things change you have the bare minimum you know needs to be done. It makes dropping a session a lot more guilt-free. Plus it gives you a weekly focus, and should stop you from overtraining in other sessions as they are not your key sessions.

5 **Experiment:** have fun playing around with your weekly volume to work out what suits you better. I found out that around 12–14 hours a week really works well for me. I did up to 17 hours, but then I always need more recovery (OK in winter, but during the summer, when racing 12–14 hours was much easier to manage).

6 **Plan your races:** a race at the end of a taper week once or twice a month can help you play around with your taper to best work out how you might improve performance.

CARL FANNON *(Australia), Dad, JBST.com iTunes podcast listener and Sprint Triathlon World Champion 35–39 London 2013*

Some great race directors make a lot for charity and their local community. They give back and they enhance. Many multi-sport athletes run an annual marathon for charity. This is not going to make you have more time but it can justify to you and others why you 'need' to get out the door and train. Charity events are done by many of my athletes – from cycling the whole length of Wales and back, to swimming challenges they would really rather not do but the charity gets them doing something for someone else 'despite' choosing the sport they had last on their list of choices. It gives balance to their normal personal focus and means they can switch off the racer in them and do something for 'a bigger reason'. Time is *not* the focus; the end result of raising cash and awareness is.

I will say no more than let the following list be a nudge to be reminded of things, many of which were given to me by clients. Sometimes, balance is about thinking what it's like to be *off*-balance:

1 The Ironman can be obsessive and all about 'more-is-better' while leaving individuals with less balance in their lives. At the time, the single-mindedness seems perfectly normal behaviour.

2 Broken friendships, divorces and business problems can stem from setting the personal performance bar way higher than reality allows. Triathlon, like many endurance sports, prides itself on focus and obsessiveness.

3 Looking at others in terms of marathon time or percentage of fat is to believe that one's sports ability is the be-all and end-all. People who save

lives every day or make others' lives bearable do not have these skills through only training for triathlon. Yet they make the world a better place but may never cross a finishing line.

4   Keeping in balance, rewarding those who support you and being 'more than tri' is a characteristic that many professional athletes possess. It's the obsessed amateur who lacks all three attributes – often as a result of 'really' wanting to be good.

5   Use single sport vacations from triathlon to keep a longer career in the sport. Many athletes go 'single-sport' for a year to go back to fun and to switch off the triathlete in them for a while. It extends their pleasure range. You've not signed up to have to race triathlon for the rest of your life.

My Last Word

From the boy who loved to run cross-country, play football and basically just ride a BMX bike (ideally just on the back wheel), or my 5-speed 'racer', for as far as my imagination would carry me, alongside my twin brother 'Snig', to racing and helping athletes do Kona, Worlds and tons of other events, I feel privileged to have been able to visit great places, learn from wonderful people and help many athletes of all levels. It is still a dream job that has made me so happy. Every day. OK, most every day.

I am enjoying multisport thirty years after starting to train formally to be a triathlete. May this book help you be the best time-crunched triathlete you can be.

To have the time, energy and money to be able to do endurance sports is a fortunate position that many on the planet will sadly never experience. In part we must never forget that and, in our own ways, be able to help others less fortunate to be able to experience some joy or respite in their challenges.

Triathlon is merely one of the vehicles in life that help people find out about themselves and others. I hope it is fair to say that triathlon has made me a better human being. I will keep trying. I will keep reading this last paragraph.

'No more than was fun to do'

'Six months before the event my base fitness was OK but my maximum distances in each discipline were 1 mile open water swim, 35 mile ride and 6 mile run. My need was to increase these distances significantly while at the same time doing no more than was necessary, no more than was wise to avoid injury and no more than was fun to do. I needed to be confident that each session was the best use of my time to achieve those aims.

The aerobic training regime Joe gave me was effective for me because it was achievable in terms of its time requirement with a little planning around my work and family schedules. It was easy in terms of intensity of effort – I felt all the activities at that intensity level would, with practice and fuelling, be capable of being stretched to the required time/distance for the event. The low intensity allowed me to literally enjoy the journey of each run, ride and swim, giving good 'me time'. It was a start to the day that I looked forward to because it was not hard or intense.

The whole idea of settling in to a rhythm that you could maintain for a long time helped me cover the long distances of Ironman because it became about replicating the process and enjoying the 'ride' rather than thinking about the (large) distance. I prepared to execute strategies to deal with any really tough moments. I learned to make good, sensible decisions through the race by engraining principles that I could call on even when exhausted.

The JBST feeding strategy was a key element to weave into the training as the times and distances increased, little by little. It developed into a simple, straightforward plan that could be applied to any distance. Practising this during training gave me real confidence that I would always be well fuelled on race-day, taking one more variable out of the equation.

Ultimately, even on the time-limited training schedule, I went into race-day confident about my preparation. I then progressed through the race with the fundamentals of fitness, fuelling and attitude that brought me home tired but healthy in under fourteen hours.'

JOHN RATLEDGE, *Ironman UK finisher 2015s and Ironman Barcelona 12 hour 50 minutess*

JOURNEY THAT ENDS IN A HOLIDAY TO REMEMBER

On the travelling and racing side, living down in Penzance (6 miles from Land's End) means being able to keep prices down on race trips and holidays. I stitch it in with a British-based mini-break. So, for example, with London tri my family and friends who also do tri and have partners (wives) that they need to keep sweet, will go from a race and move onto something like Center Parcs for a fun group break – this keeps all the family on-side and saves on travel costs.

Plus, I convinced my wife that training for Ironman Florida would end in a family holiday to remember in Disneyland, so long-term goals achieved for us all.

Also on the weekend when I have a long ride, Gin and I will plan a day out for after the ride. So I will ride to that destination – be it the beach, kids play parks, shopping, leisure facilities, etc – and they meet me there with a bag of clothes to change into. Which saves time on them sitting around waiting for me to get home, then setting off sometime in the early afternoon. A good example was earlier in the year when we took the girls to the zoo in Newquay, approximately 35 miles away. I left early and they caught me up.

BLAINE KEAREY, *Dad, sub-5-hour Etonman and 10 hour 33 minutes Florida Ironman 2013*

APPENDIX ONE

Sample Training Schedules

A plan is your coach's good guess at what you might need to do at each stage of the year. The plan will always need personalization, but it should give you the broad concepts to follow and some boundaries to stay within. The reasons why a plan tends to work is because it:

- stops you suddenly overloading in volume or intensity – your body develops gradually and so should training load
- lets you relax and not think 'where can I do more, and more?' – this means you get a training effect with lower mental stress in the background
- puts something personal to you (N = 1) on paper that you can adapt and juggle – this beats the 'I'll see what the club are doing', which adds to input from too many others (N = 5 to 25)

Use these as a source of ideas to help you look at your own situation, and move things around when the training monotony would otherwise make you go off the rails. Whatever you do, keep it simple – learn as you go what works for you, and what others can teach you.

Once you get to the season things change: you have to adapt to recovery from race weekends, time trial efforts or interval sessions twice a week take priority and the move to race specifics with equipment and venue alters what you can do and when (e.g. open water wetsuit swims, race bike rides, single-sport time trials). In season, look for recovery and good numbers from the hard work – move away from the volume and day-to-day training that winter and spring have as their MO.

The following pages show an off-season three-month plan (approx. October/November to December/January) for Months 1 to 3, followed by a pre-season training plan for three months (January to March).

Off-season 3-month plan: Month 1

	Week 1	Week 2	Week 3	Adaption Week
Mon	**SWIM** Using fins and small paddles for hand pathway focus + DWR 20 minutes	**SWIM** Using central snorkel to focus on still head, hand entry and catch phase + DWR 30 minutes	**SWIM** Pull-kick board to vary arm/leg focus + DWR 20 minutes	**SWIM** Every drill you can muster up done at least five times. Look to challenge yourself to do things right or do them until you get them right
Tue	**BIKE** 60 minutes commute, turbo or rollers + run for 10 minutes	**BIKE** 60 minutes commute, turbo or rollers + run for 10 minutes	**RUN** After 10-minute warm-up, run course for roughly 30 minutes in length, nose-breathing to keep HR <=80% (note time and average HR)	**BIKE** 60 minutes commute, turbo or rollers + run for 10 minutes
Wed	**STRENGTH TRAINING** + light run < 20 mins	**STRENGTH TRAINING** + light run < 20 mins	**STRENGTH TRAINING** + light run < 20 mins	**STRENGTH TRAINING** + light run < 20 mins
Thurs	**WEAKEST SPORT** Good technique and working on being efficient	**RUN** Your choice of time and route	**WEAKEST SPORT** Good technique and work on being efficient	**SWIM** Coached Masters, tri or fitness swim session
Fri	**NO TRAINING** Have a massage booked	**NO TRAINING** Update your SWOT list & get an early night	**NO TRAINING** Spend an hour getting your bike ship-shape	**NO TRAINING** Review your month and plan ahead
Sat	**BIKE + RUN** 1 hour flat terrain + run for 10 minutes – favourite loop enjoying riding and being relaxed	**BIKE + RUN** 1.5 hour flat terrain + run for 20 minutes	**BIKE** 1 hour 15 minutes rolling course: seated climbs (50–60 rpm bigger gear) and soft pedalling flat/descents + run 30	**BIKE + RUN** 1 hour flat terrain + run for 10 minutes
Sun	**YOUR CHOICE**	**BIKE** Check & measure set-up – easy ride after to assess	**YOUR CHOICE**	**RUN** Favourite loop

Off-season 3-month plan: Month 2

	Week 5	**Week 6**	**Week 7**	**Adaption Week**
Mon	**SWIM** Use small paddles for hand pathway focus + DWR 20 minutes	**SWIM** Central snorkel to focus on weakest side of catch + DWR 30 minutes	**SWIM** Pull-kick board to vary arm/leg focus + DWR 30 minutes	**SWIM** Favourite drills – do it right or do them again
Tue	**BIKE** 60 minutes commute, turbo or rollers + run 10 minutes	**BIKE** 80 minutes commute, turbo or rollers + run 20 minutes	**RUN** After 10-minute warm-up, run course roughly 30 minutes in length, nose-breathing to keep HR <=80% – note time and average HR	**RUN** 35–45 minutes, choosing an off-road course and keeping aerobic and smooth + turbo/gym bike spin for 15 minutes after
Wed	**RUN** For as long as a 10k tri run split takes (or twice 5k split) Aim for relaxed running with 1 minute walk every 8–10 minutes	**STRENGTH TRAINING** + easy cycle/swim <20 minutes	**BIKE** Turbo, rollers or pan-flat terrain Keep controlled in endurance zone for 60–80 minutes	**STRENGTH TRAINING** + light run <20 minutes
Thurs	**STRENGTH TRAINING** + light run <20 minutes	**RUN** Your choice of time and route	**STRENGTH TRAINING** + light run <20 minutes	**BENCHMARK** Anything from a short time trial to a looped run or turbo bike test
Fri	**NO TRAINING** Have a massage booked	**NO TRAINING** Update race plans and goals	**NO TRAINING** Organize kit – can you reduce some old, unused or ineffective items?	**NO TRAINING** Review your month – what are your weakest or most threatening factors?
Sat	**BIKE** 1.25 hour flat terrain + run 10 minutes on favourite loop enjoying riding and being relaxed	**BIKE** 1.75 hour flat terrain + run 25 minutes	**BIKE** 1.25 hour rolling course: seated climbs (50–60 rpm bigger gear) and soft pedalling either flat or descents + run 35 minutes	**NO TRAINING** **NO TRIATHLON** **EAT VARIED**
Sun	**SOMETHING NEW** For example, ride with friends on a new route or in a new group, and enjoy being able to draft	**CROSS TRAIN** Try something different or new – except turn down your competitive psyche	**CROSS TRAIN** Try something different or new	**YOUR CHOICE**

Off-season 3-month plan: Month 3

	Week 9	**Week 10**	**Week 11**	**Adaption Week**
Mon	**SWIM** Masters or tri session	**SWIM** Masters or tri session	**SWIM** Masters or tri session	**SWIM** Masters or tri session (drop back in lane to reduce effort)
Tue	**BIKE** 60 minutes commute, turbo or rollers. + run 10 minutes	**RUN** After 10-minute warm-up, run course roughly 30 minutes in length while nose-breathing to keep HR <=80% Note time and average HR	**RUN** Your choice of time and route	**BIKE** 60 minutes commute, turbo or rollers + run 20 minutes
Wed	**STRENGTH TRAINING** + light run < 20 minutes	**STRENGTH TRAINING** + light run < 20 minutes	**STRENGTH TRAINING** + light run < 20 minutes	**STRENGTH TRAINING** + light run < 20 minutes
Thurs	**NO TRAINING** Have a sports or self-massage for 30–60 minutes	**OPPORTUNITY** Extra session in your least done sport	**OPPORTUNITY** Extra session with a friend you don't normally get to train with	**RUN** Your choice of time and route
Fri	**NO TRAINING** Update race plans and goals	**NO TRAINING** Organize kit – can you reduce some old, unused or ineffective items?	**NO TRAINING** Organize a blood profile test for next week	**OPPORTUNITY** Any aerobic sport just make it fun
Sat	**BIKE + RUN (x 2)** 30–40 minutes flat (or indoors) + run 10 minutes	**BIKE + RUN** 2 hour flat terrain + run 10–20 minutes	**BIKE + RUN** 1.5 hour flat terrain + run 25–30 minutes	**NO TRAINING** OK, a short session (if you really want to) but tomorrow is off totally
Sun	**YOUR CHOICE**	**RUN** After 10-minute warm-up, run course roughly 30 minutes in length while nose-breathing to keep HR <=80% – note time and average HR	**CROSS TRAIN** Try something different or new – except turn down your competitive psyche	**NO TRAINING**

Pre-season 3-month plan: Month 1

	Week 1	Week 2	Week 3	Adaption Week
Mon	**SWIM** Masters or tri session	**SWIM** Masters or tri session – include a swim time trial benchmark	**SWIM** Masters or tri session	**SWIM** Masters or tri session Drop a lane (but not the front) to focus on a smooth consistent stroke
Tue	**BIKE** 60 minutes commute, turbo periods of 3–5 minutes on aerobars + run 15 minutes	**TURBO BRICK** 1 hour 10 minutes 2 × turbo with race bike for 15 minutes in Zone 1, with alternating 5 minutes on/off aerobars, then 20 minutes run	**BIKE** 70 minutes commute, turbo periods of 3–5 minutes on aerobars + run 15–30 minutes	**TURBO BRICK** 1 hour 15 minutes 3 × turbo with race bike for 15 minutes in Zone 1, with alternating 1 minute on/off aerobars, then 10 minute run
Wed	**STRENGTH TRAINING** + light run 20 minutes	**STRENGTH TRAINING** + light swim 20–30 minutes	**STRENGTH TRAINING** + light run < 20 minutes	**STRENGTH TRAINING** + light swim 20–30 minutes
Thurs	**SWIM** 45 minutes Choose to repeat on group session from past month	**RUN** After 10-minute warm-up, run course roughly 30 minutes in length while nose-breathing to keep HR <=80% Note time and average HR	**MISSED SPORT?** Check back last two weeks and use this session to focus on good technique in the sport most neglected	**CROSS TRAIN** Try something different or new – except turn down your competitive psyche
Fri	**NO TRAINING** Update race plans and goals	**NO TRAINING** Organize kit – can you reduce some old, unused or ineffective items?	**SWIM** Warm up for 15 minutes + swim 50–75% of race distance at best speed you can hold Note time and reappraise speed, endurance and pacing abilities	**NO TRAINING** Admin for 1 hour + organize swim bag, service bike, nutrition supplies acquired, etc.
Sat	**BIKE + RUN** 2 hour flat terrain + run 15 minutes + drills: 4 × 60–70 metres with jog-back recovery of high knees, fast feet, bottom kicks and bounding	**BIKE + RUN** 1 hour 30 minutes rolling course in one gear higher/harder (i.e. smaller) than before with seated climbs + 15 minute run + drill: 4 × 60–70 metres	**NO TRAINING**	**BIKE+ RUN** 1 hour 20 minutes flat terrain + run 10 minutes with relaxed leg turnover
Sun	Favourite 1-hour session	**MISSED SESSION** Whatever high-priority session has been missed in the last 2 weeks – do it now	**MISSED SESSION** Whatever high-priority session has been missed in the last 2 weeks – do it now	

Pre-season 3-month plan: Month 2

	Week 5	Week 6	Week 7	Adaption Week
Mon	**SWIM** Masters or tri session	**SWIM** Masters or tri session	**SWIM** Masters or tri session – include a swim time trial (perhaps wetsuit?) benchmark	**SWIM** Masters or tri session Drop a lane to focus on achieving a smooth consistent stroke
Tue	**BIKE** 60–70 minutes commute, turbo periods of 5–8 minutes on aerobars + 15-minute run	**TURBO BRICK** 1 hour 20 minutes: 4 × turbo with race bike for 10 minutes in Zone 1, with alternating 2 minute on/off aerobars, then 10-minute run	**BIKE** 60 minutes commute, turbo periods of 5 minutes on aerobars + 25-minute run	**TURBO BRICK** 1 hour 3 × turbo with race bike for 10 minutes in Zone 1, with alternating 2 minutes on/off aerobars, then 10-minute run
Wed	**STRENGTH TRAINING** + light swim for 20 minutes	**STRENGTH TRAINING** + light swim for 20–30 minutes	**STRENGTH TRAINING ONLY**	**STRENGTH TRAINING ONLY**
Thurs	**YOUR CHOICE**	**RUN** After 10-minute warm up, run relaxed for 30–55 minutes Vary terrain and keep relaxed, with economical form	**YOUR CHOICE**	**RUN** After 10-minute warm-up, run relaxed for 30–45 minutes Vary terrain and keep relaxed, with economical form
Fri	**RUN** After 10-minute warm-up, run relaxed for 30–5 minutes Vary terrain and keep relaxed, with economical form	**NO TRAINING** Update race plans and goals	**NO TRAINING** Organize kit – can you reduce some old, unused or ineffective items?	**NO TRAINING** Ideally have a sports massage
Sat	**BIKE + RUN** 2 hour 25 minutes on flat terrain + 15-minute run + drills: 4 × 60–70 metres with jog-back recovery of high knees, fast feet, bottom kicks and bounding	**BIKE** 1 hour rolling course with seated climbs + 10-minute run + drills: 4 × 60–70 metre drills	**NO TRAINING**	**BIKE + RUN** 1 hour 30 minutes on very flat terrain (or indoors) + run for 10 minutes with relaxed leg turnover
Sun	**RUN** 20 minutes relaxed warm-up + 20-minute drills, 4 × 60–70 metres with jog-back recovery of high knees, fast feet, bottom kicks and bounding + 3–5 minutes skipping	**TRI DAY** Swim 30 minutes fitness session with 8 × 100 main set off 30 second rest Bike either in gym or back home on rollers (or turbo) for 30-minute spin + 15-minute run on treadmill or flat terrain at cruise pace but relaxed	**TRI DAY** Swim 30 minutes fitness session with 8 × 100 main set-off with 30-second rest + bike either in gym or back home on rollers (or turbo) for 40-minute spin + 20-minute run on treadmill or flat terrain at cruise pace but relaxed	**TRI DAY** Swim 30 minutes fitness session with 10 × 100 main set-off with 60-second rest + bike either in gym or back home on rollers (or turbo) for 50-minute spin + 20-minute run on treadmill or flat terrain at cruise pace but relaxed

Pre-season 3-month plan: Month 3

	Week 9	Week 10	Week 11	Adaption Week
Mon	NO TRAINING	SWIM Masters or tri session	SWIM Masters or tri session	SWIM Masters or tri session – include a swim time trial (perhaps wetsuit?) benchmark
Tue	TURBO BRICK 50 minutes 2 × turbo with race bike for 20 minutes in Zone 1 + 5-minute run with fast-feet tempo and shortened stride + back to bike	TURBO BRICK 1 hour 20 minutes 4 × turbo with race bike for 10 minutes in Zone 1, with alternating 2 minutes on/off aerobars + 10-minute run	TURBO BRICK 1 hour 20 minutes 4 × turbo with race bike for 10 minutes in Zone 1, with alternating 2 minutes on/off aerobars + 10-minute run	TURBO BRICK 50 minutes 2 × turbo with race bike for 20 minutes in Zone 1 + 5-minute run with fast-feet tempo and shortened stride + back to bike
Wed	STRENGTH TRAINING + light swim for 20 minutes	STRENGTH TRAINING + light swim for 20–30 minutes	STRENGTH TRAINING ONLY	STRENGTH TRAINING ONLY
Thurs	RUN After 10-minute warm-up, run relaxed for 30–55 minutes Vary terrain and keep relaxed, with economical form	YOUR CHOICE	RUN After 10-minute warm-up, run relaxed for 30–45 minutes Vary terrain and keep relaxed, with economical form	BIKE 1 hour to 1 hour 20 minutes soft pedalling – gym, rollers, turbo or extra commute time
Fri	BIKE 1 hour to 1 hour 20 minutes soft pedalling – gym, rollers, turbo or extra commute time	SWIM 45–60 minutes including 125% of your target triathlon swim (continuous) Don't watch the clock; cruise while keeping strokes controlled, but do note your time + 5-minute cool-down	NO TRAINING Update race plans and goals Organize a blood profiling test for next week	SWIM Warm-up Swim 50–75% of race distance at best speed you can hold Note time and reappraise speed, endurance and pacing abilities
Sat	NO TRAINING	BIKE + RUN 2 hour flat terrain + 15-minute run + drills: 4 × 60–70 metres with jog-back recovery of: high knees, fast feet, bottom kicks and bounding	BIKE + RUN 2 hour 30 minutes on flat terrain + 15-minute run + drills: 4 × 60–70 metres with jog-back recovery of high knees, fast feet, bottom kicks and bounding	NO TRAINING Admin for 1 hour Check nutrition, order where necessary Look for local o/w swim, time trial and run races to fill in gaps in competition and build to key races
Sun	TRI DAY Swim 30-minute fitness session with 8 ×100 main set-off with 30-second rest Bike either in gym or back home on rollers (or turbo) for 30-minute spin + 15-minute run on treadmill or flat terrain at cruise pace but relaxed	TRI DAY Swim 30 minutes fitness session with 8 ×100 main set-off with 30-second rest Bike either in gym or back home on rollers (or turbo) for 40-minute spin + 20-minute run on treadmill or flat terrain at cruise pace but relaxed	NO TRAINING	TRI DAY Swim 30-minute fitness session with 12 ×100 main set-off with 30-second rest Bike either in gym or back home on rollers (or turbo) for 60-minute spin + 30-minute run on treadmill or flat terrain at cruise pace but relaxed

APPENDIX TWO

Your Toolbox for Future Success

A book on triathlon shouldn't be something you read just once, then put back on the shelf to gather dust – and *Time-Crunched Triathlon* is definitely not that sort of book. *Time-Crunched Triathlon* is a log of essential information about triathlon and about *you*. It is a key reference tool for you to read and refer to again and again. And, as you read it and grow in experience, you can add to it with every piece of new information you find. Every time you re-read a specific chapter to deal with your current situation, you can add further experience and solutions, building up your triathlete tool kit as you go along.

So, here are the essential tools for your future time-crunch challenges. No one has infinite time; no one can afford to be training randomly. There are those that keep their books pristine, others scribble, highlight and slip articles inside a growing tome. Use *Time-Crunched Triathlon* as you wish – write on it, photocopy the forms in it, but do use it. The forms here may take a few minutes to fill in, but this investment of only a few minutes will help you to become a better triathlete in the longer run, so get scribbling!

SWOT

Think not only about training and racing, but also about your general diet, sports nutrition use, work, family, etc. Try to be balanced in finding strengths, weaknesses, opportunities and threats, and – most importantly – be honest with yourself.

Strengths

What gives me a positive mindset and appears to be a natural ability?

SWIM

BIKE

RUN

NUTRITION

EQUIPMENT

ORGANIZATION & ADMINISTRATION

FAMILY & WORK

Weaknesses

What makes me feel negative about myself and my performances?

SWIM

....

....

BIKE

....

....

RUN

....

....

NUTRITION

....

....

EQUIPMENT

....

....

ORGANIZATION & ADMINISTRATION

....

....

FAMILY & WORK

....

....

Opportunities

What factors (e.g. time, terrain, friends, group sessions) give rise to me doing things more efficiently, more effectively or more consistently?

SWIM

....

....

BIKE

....

....

RUN

....

....

NUTRITION

....

....

EQUIPMENT

....

....

ORGANIZATION & ADMINISTRATION

....

....

FAMILY & WORK

....

....

Threats

What factors (e.g. injuries, lack of balance) could put my health, training or racing in jeopardy?

SWIM
....
....

BIKE
....
....

RUN
....
....

NUTRITION
....
....

EQUIPMENT
....
....

ORGANIZATION & ADMINISTRATION
....
....

FAMILY & WORK
....
....
....

Swot Analysis

Activity	Strengths	Weaknesses	Opportunities	Threats
All training				
Daily diet & sports nutrition usage				
All equipment				
Race performances				
Work & family commitments				

Heart Rate Training Zones

Use this page to ensure that you have your zones up to date using race, training and max test data and to ensure you are training honestly.

Name and %HRmax	Description	My Numbers
HR Maximum 100%	Absolute hardest effort possible unlikely to be in race, e.g. maximum test on bike	
Zone 3: Lactate accumulation 88–99%	Hard-race pace effort and intervals or hills in training, e.g. 3 × 8 minutes, with 10 minutes of recovery in between (Zone 1 effort)	
Zone 2: Lactate accumulation 81–87%	Harder training effort and race pace cruising, e.g. 70.3 tri, out of hand group ride, run endurance session that turns to a race	
Zone1: Low lactate 50%–80%	Endurance building zone Health benefits are enormous, e.g. 2 hour bike, 45 minutes run	

Food Diary

Use this page to ensure that you have your zones up to date using race, training and max test data and to ensure you are training honestly.

Day	Breakfast	Lunch	Dinner	Snacks	Training Type & Quality of Sessions
Sun					
Mon					
Tue					
Wed					
Thur					
Fri					
Sat					

Swim Stroke Feedback

Jot down any feedback on your stroke mechanics from video analysis, your coach's poolside comments or the input from significant 'others'.

DATE .... OBSERVER ....

Point 1

COMMENT: ....

BODY PART: ....

ERROR: ....

WHAT DRILLS TO DO: ....

REMINDER: ....

TOOLS TO USE: ....

Point 2

COMMENT: ....

BODY PART: ....

ERROR: ....

WHAT DRILLS TO DO: ....

REMINDER: ....

TOOLS TO USE: ....

Point 3

COMMENT:

....

BODY PART:

....

ERROR:

....

WHAT DRILLS TO DO:

....

REMINDER:

....

TOOLS TO USE:

....

OVERALL:

....

COMMENTS AND REMINDERS:

....

....

....

....

....

....

....

....

My Best Training Sessions

When you read and/or try a great session, or perhaps use a session before races to good effect, jot down how you do them best – these are your sessions that work, i.e. your best training sessions.

SESSION NAME:
....

NOTES:
....

....

....

BENEFITS FROM SESSION:
....

....

....

WARM-UP:
....

MAIN SESSION:
....

COOL-DOWN:
....

RECOVERY (SORTED OUT BEFOREHAND):
....

....

Weight Training Tips

Always warm up (row/cycle at steady Zone 1 effort for 5–12 minutes) and cool down after (easy row/cycle + light (hold for 30 seconds) stretching for 5–10 minutes).

Use a copy of this form on page 222 and fill out:

- your resistance (kilograms, pounds or number on machine)
- your repetitions
- your rate of perceived exertion (RPE)
- any additional exercises for your imbalances/injuries.

Drink 60 grams of carbohydrate + 25 grams of protein + 5 grams of creatine during + carb + protein 'real' food 1–2 hour after (e.g. tuna, jacket potato and salad).

Every third session reverse the order of exercises.

Use good form and controlled breathing throughout session.

Rest 2–3 minutes between hard sets.

Keep sessions less than 60 minutes two days apart and minimize endurance training of more than 60 minutes on a weights day.

In the gym you need to be precise in the exercise, exercise load and progression you ask of your body. To get stronger in tune with your body use page 222 to plan and track the exercises and resistances that you use.

Resistance Training Diary

NAME
....

Periodization (month/year)	Oct	Nov	Dec	Jan	Feb	Mar	Apr	May+
Sessions per week (30–55 mins each)	1–2	2	2	2–3	2–3	2–3	2	1–2
No. of sets × reps	2x12	1x2 1x12RM	1x12 1x10–12RM	1x12 2x10RM	1x12 2x10RM	1x12 2x8–10RM	1x12 2x10RM	1x2 1x10–12RM
RESISTANCE EXERCISE		RESISTANCE USED IN SESSIONS BELOW						
1 Lat pull-down (seated/bent row)								
2 Single-leg leg press (one-leg squats)								
3 Calf raise (bench/ box step-ups)								
4 Triceps press-down (triceps kickback)								
5 Half squat (hack squat – heel raised)								
6 Hip flexion (Roman chair leg raise)								
7 DB lateral/front/45° raise (upright row)								
8 One-leg leg press (bent leg deadlift)								
9 Bench crunches (DB oblique sidebends)								

RM = repetition maximum, e.g. 10RM means 'total fatigue on tenth rep'

Smart Training Checklist

This list keeps track of your actions, kit and admin tasks to help you be the most time-efficient high performer you can be. Some of this may be irrelevant to you (if so, simply ignore it). Other elements will be vital, so highlight these and be sure to check back to keep yourself super-effective in all that you do.

To be admin-efficient is to train smart, so come back to this once a month and update.

Essentials

Decide priority (A) race, building (B) and completion (C) events or goals . . . . ☐

Plan 1 hour per month for admin & race planning/entry . . . . ☐

Add race details, e.g. location, distances, terrain, temperatures, start time,
to your race planner (see pages 236–8) . . . . ☐

Keep concise diary and review monthly:
▪ are you doing 70–90 per cent in Zone 1 & skill? . . . . ☐
▪ + 10–20 per cent in Zones 2 and 3 + strength work? . . . . ☐
▪ Track your body weight and body fat level (if a 'Weakness', do this fortnightly) . . . . ☐

Slow warm-ups for 15–20 minutes in Zone 1 for every session
(especially for Zone 2/Zone 3 intervals, group sessions and races) . . . . ☐

Light box use in training/on desk at work in mornings + any lunchtime sessions
(use Lumie Bodyclock alarm in winter) . . . . ☐

Compression clothing used after hard sessions and races (first 3–24 hours are vital)
especially when in cold conditions afterwards. . . . . ☐

Use colostrum 10–20 grams per day for health, immune strength and lean mass . . . . ☐

Good hand hygiene at home, work and when travelling (i.e. washing with hand gel) . . . . . . ☐

Blood profiling every 3–6 months (early off-season, mid-winter, pre-season,
mid-competition season), e.g. InDurance.co.uk . . . . ☐

Swim

Swimming planned 2–4 days per week (coached, masters or solo sessions
with session printed (i.e. wetsuit, drafting practice, skills focus & endurance) . . . . ☐
    Pack swim bag with:
- spare goggles . . . . ☐
- hat . . . . ☐
- costume . . . . ☐
- towel . . . . ☐
- money . . . . ☐
- energy drink sachet/gel . . . . ☐

Wetsuit use once a week from January to September . . . . ☐

Plan time trials, distance and/or stroke-count tests . . . . ☐

Vasa workouts for swim-specific strength . . . . ☐

Swim bands to practise warm-ups for races . . . . ☐

Resistance bands for resistance work when travelling . . . . ☐

Add Deep Water Running (DWR) to swim sessions to increase endurance
and reduce run impact (two sports with a fast change required) . . . . ☐

At 4–6 weeks open-water acclimation:
- race starts . . . . ☐
- cold water practice . . . . ☐
- wetsuit off and DryRobe changing routine (from May onwards) . . . . ☐

Open-water drafting practice (both sides breathing) and wetsuit dressing time
(i.e. how to put on suit correctly and in a relaxed manner) . . . . ☐

Cycle

Emergency spares at home:
- three tubes . . . . ☐
- tyre . . . . ☐
- rim tape . . . . ☐
- wheelset . . . . ☐
- batteries . . . . ☐
- chain . . . . ☐
- cleats . . . . ☐

Cycle(s) insured and policy up to date . . . . ☐

Correct bike fit and comfortable aero-position . . . . ☐
- measurement of final position . . . . ☐
- attachment of, and practice with, aerobars – even using rollers as an advanced
training technique . . . . ☐

Turbo trainer with race bike: include year-round over-geared riding
(e.g. 3 x 8 minutes @ 60 rpm on aerobars) . . . . ☐

Fixed-gear rides (pick a gear and go!) also road muscle tension
(50–60 rpm inclines for 4–8 minutes) – spinning 90+ rpm between and afterwards . . . . . ☐

Inclusion of bike-handling (experienced group ride?), including:
- descents . . . . ☐
- corners . . . . ☐
- draft-legal practice . . . . ☐
- repeated technical descent practice . . . . ☐

Aero helmet, tight fitting trisuit/skinsuit, tri shoes, arm coolers/warmer options
for racing . . . . □

Aero wheels with 40–90 millimetre rim depth, low-rolling resistance tyres/tubs
(e.g. Continental GP4000 S II 25mm) and a lubed chain . . . . □

Drink options/position, optimized accessories, spare tube/tub,
PIT'STOP or similar, CO_2, etc . . . . □

Race pace practice in time trials and shorter triathlons/duathlons
with POWER/HR data reviewed for pace awareness . . . . □

Run

Low-impact mixed terrain 2–4 days per week (incl. DWR) with a Double-Run Session
Day (DRSD) . . . . □

Purchased DWR belt . . . . □

Treadmill and/or looped test monthly (e.g. 3–5 miles at 75–80% HRmax
to assess efficiency/fitness) . . . . □

1–2 brick sessions weekly (after long cycle, over-geared cycle or turbo over-geared work)
10–40 minutes running . . . . □

Hill training – short power bursts (20–50 metres) or long endurance hills
(3–8 minutes at upper Zone 2 or Zone 3) – with soft surface long-way-down recoveries . . □

Use of stepper for low-impact strength and treadmill on incline . . . . □

Technique work (track, treadmill with mirror) within/or at end of every run
(e.g. 8 × 100 metres at 5k pace with jog recoveries between) . . . . □

Recovery drink or milkshake – in or after long runs over 60 minutes
and any Zone 2/Zone 3 intense runs or races . . . . □

Use calf supports during run training, recovery from run training or when
stood on your feet for several hours, flights (e.g. CEP run sock) . . . . □

Your race shoes tried and tested, e.g. fit, etc – perhaps add lace locks to training shoes
as well to save time and make their use second nature . . . . □

Nutrition, Mind & Racing

Fluid replacement and race-day energy sources tried and tested
(e.g. pre-caffeine; pre-carbs; in-event feeding, and post recovery) . . . . ☐

Meditation and relaxation at-home sessions once per week (e.g. for 20 minutes
to clear head and focus on goal and present habits/barriers . . . . ☐

Massage/chiropractic/reflexology/Bowen – once every 2–6 weeks
(with emergency experts' numbers/contact details noted) . . . . ☐

Regular review of training–racing–work–home balance to ensure harmony . . . . ☐

Caffeine, refined sugar, alcohol, personal allergens (CRAP) detox in the off-season
and, possibly, for some the 7–14 days before your big 'A' races . . . . ☐

Pre-race breakfast, warm-up dialled-in
(e.g. swim cordz, turbo trainer and/or short run drills) . . . . ☐

Pre-race 'loading' and pre-hydration routine tried and tested
(e.g. 4 days of carbo-loading) . . . . ☐

One or two 10–20 minute sessions per week to visualize good race performances
– possibly while stretching in cool-down . . . . ☐

Advanced Performance

Training zones & metabolic assessment, e.g. www.trainsmart.com .... ☐

Attend training days, presentations & warm-weather training camps .... ☐

Track Aero – assessment of position, clothing and equipment, e.g. AeroCoach .... ☐

For when head is congested, use nasal strips for training and Olbas oil vapour
inhalation and ioniser in the bedroom .... ☐

Altitude tent hire (>1 month) or training camps (>1500 metres, 10–20+ days) .... ☐

Caffeine (1 hour pre-race/HIT/resistance sessions) approx. 100–350 milligrams .... ☐

Sodium phosphate (2 × 3d or 1 × 6d pre-race load up,
as per manufacturer's direction) .... ☐

Beetroot juice (500 millilitres juice or 2 × BEET IT for 6–14 days pre-race) .... ☐

Beta-Alanine loading (as per PowerBar.co.uk loading regime online) .... ☐

Kit Data

Use this page to record the key equipment you use other than your bike (for that, use the Bike Data form on page 232). Having the data to hand will save you time and money when you come to replace parts of your kit.

Once you have completed the form, keep it somewhere handy, and update it, as appropriate.

Kit Data Form

Swimming Goggles	Swimming Costume
Brand Model Size	Brand Model Size
Bike Shoes (Race)	**Bike Shoes (Training)**
Brand Size Any orthotics used?	Brand Size Any orthotics used?
Running Shoes (Race)	**Running Shoes (Training)**
Brand Model Size Any orthotics?	Brand Model Size Any orthotics?

Bike Data

Use the form on page 232 to record the vital statistics of your bicycle – yes, that's every bicycle you own. This is time-consuming but will save you time when you come to replace your bike or parts of it.

Take a series of measurements of your bike and add them to the **Bike Data** form on page 232. This will help you with positional changes and equipment upgrades in the event of theft or your bike being written off. It also is an injury-prevention measure when travelling, moving over to a new bike, hiring a bike or when you get lost with your 'playing with my position'.

You should:

1   Check that your bike is horizontal by using a spirit level on the top tube (assuming that the top tube is flat).
2   Have all items on the bike that you use in training or racing.
3   List your cycling shoe size, cleat position and any wedges or orthotics used.
4   Measure your training and racing bike set-ups.

You'll need a tape measure, spirit level, plumbline, paper and pen/pencil.

Once you have completed the form, keep it somewhere handy, and update it, as appropriate.

Bike Data Form

		Aerobar	
Brand		Brand	
Model		Model	
Year		**Gears**	
Frame number		Brand	
Frame size		Model	
Identification tag		Number of gears	
Seat		**Chain Ring**	
Brand		Size (e.g. 39, 53)	
Model		Rear cassette sizes (e.g. 12, 13, 14, 15, 17, 19, 21, 23, 25 and 27)	
Crank		**Tyre**	
Brand		Brand	
Model		Width (Continental GP 4000S 11700 x 25)	
Length			

Vital Measurements	
The distance from the centre of the bottom bracket to the middle of the top of the middle of the seat	
The distance between the pedal axle and the top of the middle of the seat (with the crank set at its lowest point in line with the seat tube)	
The horizontal distance from the nose of the saddle to the middle of the aerobar pads (or handlebars, if no aerobars)	
The horizontal distance from the front of the saddle to a line running vertically up from the centre of the bottom bracket – use a plumbline for accuracy	
The horizontal distance from the frontmost point of the aerobars to the centre of the aerobar pads	
The vertical distance from the aerobar pad to the floor	
The horizontal distance from the centre of the left aerobar pad to the centre of the right aerobar pad (the forearm-to-forearm measurement when in aerobar position)	
The vertical distance from the brake lever gear (axis or pulling point) to the floor	

Body Database Form

Use this form to note serious injuries, surgery and measurements as well as any niggles, signs of wear and weaknesses. Doing this will help you to track the evolution of an injury and note how you best deal with adversity when it hits.

Adversity *will* hit eventually, so make a copy of this and give it to your most regularly visited body-worker to add to their notes.

PRE SYMPTOMS

....

....

....

....

....

....

....

NOTES AFTERWARDS

....

....

....

....

....

....

....

DRAW AREAS TO FOCUS ON BELOW

Racing Checklist

This list has evolved from use by many athletes over several years. It's not foolproof, so adapt as you find necessary. Add or take items off to suit your specific circumstances/needs.

I must always remember to take ....

ADMIN

- [ ] BTF/NGB card
- [ ] Race details
- [ ] Directions to venue
- [ ] Travel insurance contact details
- [ ] Wallet
- [ ] Phone
- [ ] Phone charger
- [ ] Sunglasses
- [ ] Snack
- [ ] Drink

BIKE

- [ ] Bike & wheels
- [ ] Spare inner tubes/tyre/tub
- [ ] Track pump & turbo trainer/rollers
- [ ] Chain lube
- [ ] Allen/Hex keys
- [ ] Bento box
- [ ] Aero helmet
- [ ] Bike shoes + rubber bands
- [ ] Sports bottle

RUN TRANSITION

- [ ] Run shoes
- [ ] Run cap
- [ ] Transition towel
- [ ] Talcum powder
- [ ] Vaseline

RACE MORNING

- [ ] Tri suit
- [ ] HRM strap
- [ ] HRM watch
- [ ] Timing chip
- [ ] Sun cream
- [ ] Old spare run shoes
- [ ] Run tights
- [ ] Thermal top
- [ ] Cereal/breakfast snacks
- [ ] Spoon
- [ ] Coffee flask

SWIM START

- ☐ DryRobe
- ☐ Body glide
- ☐ Silicon swim cap
- ☐ Baby oil
- ☐ Goggle solution
- ☐ Goggles
- ☐ 2 × gel
- ☐ Old bottle of energy drink
- ☐ Race belt
- ☐ Race number
- ☐ Wet suit
- ☐ Baby wipes

FUEL

- ☐ Energy drink
- ☐ Water – 1 bottle (750 millilitres)
- ☐ Pre-race drink

POST-RACE

- ☐ Towel
- ☐ Recovery drink
- ☐ Compression tights
- ☐ Casual T-shirt
- ☐ Thermal base layer
- ☐ Jeans
- ☐ Electrolyte tablets
- ☐ Waterproof jacket

INTERNATIONAL?

- ☐ Passport
- ☐ Foreign currency
- ☐ Hotel details

Race Planner

Use this form to prepare yourself for big events by going into the kind of detail you would not ordinarily think about for small or single sport events.

Much of the kit used is in your **Racing Checklist** (see pages 234–5), but your **Race Planner** form includes pacing, nutrition regime, race details – all designed to make big events go with a bang!

EVENT NAME	
Contact Name & Number	
Travel	
Travel details (ticket references, route, etc.)	
Travel insurance details	
Accommodation	
Race Day	
Expected weather	
Time of start	
Race distance/splits	
'Failure' splits and final time	
'Adequate' splits and final time	
'Success' splits and final time	
'Dream goal' splits and final time	
Actual splits from race results	
Week Before	
Last 3 to 7 days spent training	
Diet changes	
Training at venue?	
Mental strategy/mindset	

Equipment	
Essential to pack (must not forget)	
Wetsuit/goggles	
Bike frame	
Bike wheels (tyres/width & cassette)	
Bike effort? (Power meter, HRM or RPE)	
Bike spares (wheels, tyres, etc.)	
Bike emergency pack (incl. pump)	
Running shoes/clothing/hat/belt, etc.	
Extras (old shoes for swim, T1 bottle, etc.)	
Race bags	
Swim kit & warm pre-race gear	
T1 Bag	
T2 Bag	
Nutrtion	
Hydration/food boxes	
Breakfast (tried & tested)	
Pre-hydration	
Warm-up (with caffeine)	
Notes	

Race morning timing	
At Swim Start	
Feeding	
Positioning	
Mental strategy (e.g. course direction/turns)	
On the Bike	
Feed-station positions	
Feeding	
Description of what's on offer	
Pacing	
Mental strategy	
On the Run	
Feeding frequency/intake:	
Description of what's on offer	
Pacing	
Mental Strategy	

Race Personal Bests (PBs)

List everything you can recall that has been an effort. Be honest – this is your goal post ... you on a good day ... your personal victories against the clock or other athletes.

SWIM (all distances given in metres)

400
....

750
....

1,500
....

1,900
....

3,800
....

BIKE (all distances given in kilometres)

Hill effort (e.g. Box Hill)
....

Training loop
....

20
....

40
....

90
....

180
....

RUN (all distances given in kilometres, except where specified)

Training Loop (e.g. LPR, Heanton, Po)
....

5
....

10
....

10 miles
....

21
....

42
....

TRIATHLON

Sprint

Event/Splits/Overall/AG position

Event/Splits/Overall/AG position

Olympic/standard

Event/Splits/Overall/AG position

Event/Splits/Overall/AG position

Half Ironman/Middle

Event/Splits/Overall/AG position

Event/Splits/Overall/AG position

Ironman

Event/Splits/Overall/AG position

Event/Splits/Overall/AG position

Duathlon

Event/Splits/Overall/AG position

Event/Splits/Overall/AG position

Race Post-Mortem

Complete this form soon after key events and build up the experiences on one sheet to see trends of both problems and successes.

Topic	Strong or Weak? Perfect or Opportunity?	Next Action(s)
Tapering & Travel		
Race Pacing		
Nutrition Feeding		
Race-day Equipment		

Vital Information

Here is where you keep your key contacts, websites, usernames, telephone numbers, opening times and passwords. It's the information that you're not supposed to keep in your head. You could keep it on a computer or on your smartphone. Keep this current and you're going to be much more time-efficient. No battery or software-update required!

Swimming

POOLS

Name .... Contact/tel. ....

Address: ....

....

COACHES

Name .... Contact/tel. ....

Name .... Contact/tel. ....

WEBSITES

Swimming-pool Finder (www.swimming.org/poolfinder)

Bike

SHOPS

Name .... Contact/tel. ....

Name .... Contact/tel. ....

CLUBS

Name .... Contact/tel. ....

Name .... Contact/tel. ....

WEBSITES

Running

CLUBS

Name .... Contact/tel. ....

Name .... Contact/tel. ....

GYM

Name .... Contact/tel. ....

Name .... Contact/tel. ....

COACH

Name .... Contact/tel. ....

Name .... Contact/tel. ....

Experts

MASSEUSE

Name .... Contact/tel. ....

BOWEN PRACTITIONER

Name .... Contact/tel. ....

CHIROPRACTOR

Name   Contact/tel. ....

PHYSIO(S)

Name .... Contact/tel. ....

Name .... Contact/tel. ....

SWIM CLUB

Name .... Contact/tel. ....

Name .... Contact/tel. ....

BIKE CLUB

Name .... Contact/tel. ....

Name .... Contact/tel. ....

RUN CLUB

Name .... Contact/tel. ....

Name .... Contact/tel. ....

TRIATHLON CLUB

Name .... Contact/tel. ....

Name .... Contact/tel. ....

YOUR TOOLBOX FOR FUTURE SUCCESS

Login Details

STRAVA

User name .... password ....

GARMIN

User name .... password ....

MAGAZINE (specify)

User name .... password ....

OTHER (specify)

User name .... password ....

OTHER (specify)

User name .... password ....

OTHER (specify)

User name .... password ....

Equipment & Services for Triathletes

www.220triathlon.com
Bestselling and longest running UK triathlon magazine *220 Triathlon* with articles, videos, reviews and myTRI training log

www.speedo.co.uk
Speedo UK is a brand synonymous with swimming, but also central to the DNA of triathlon clothing, wetsuits, goggles and training aids

www.swimfortri.com
Swim For TriExperts offers information to help triathletes swim faster, more efficiently and with a better understanding of swimming technique

www.vasatrainer.com
Provides access to blog and details of equipment to improve your swim strength, technique and testing

www.scott-sports.com
Provides newletter, videos and information about aero road and tri bikes, high spec cycling shoes and run shoes – also clothing of the highest standard and comfort

www.vervecycling.com
Provides super-stiff, industry-leading accurate InfoCranks to measure power, left-right balance, and many other efficiency metrics whilst temperature steady and very durable.

www.pedalcover.co.uk
Insurance cover for training and competing home or abroad under a simple single home insurance policy

www.ctt.org.uk
Helps you to find cycling club and time trials, with the inside-track on everything about UK time trialling

www.nopinz.com
Innovative solutions to number placement, multi-sport clothing and aerodynamic cycle products

www.powerbar.eu/en
Source of information about nutrition, events and energy products

www.neovite.com
Provides information about colostrum and the science for this nutritional aid

www.InDurance.co.uk
Blood-profiling service for all levels of athlete to reveal the internal status of vitamins, hormones and blood efficiency to maximize your fitness, performance and recovery

www.dryrobe.com

Information and the ability to buy the ultimate change robe that is perfect for pre-multi-sport races, after cold swims, and morning sportives to evening running events

www.lumie.com

News and information about light boxes that help you to cope with early morning and mid-winter blues as well as change of time zones, in the home, gym or office

www.trainsmart.com

Online training resource for athletes and coaches to plan, analyse and get help with training for all types of endurance event

www.bit.ly/JBSTpod

Monthly podcast (available free to members) on iTunes since 2006; includes questions & answers, tips, advice and top athlete interviews

www.fx-sport.co.uk

Details about innovative headphones designed for sportspeople, with professional coaching audio workouts and motivational instruction to maximize swim, bike, run and gym training sessions

Endnotes

Chapter 5 Ten Effective Training Sessions

1 Adapted from Barnes *et al.*, 'Effects of different uphill interval-training programs on running economy and performance', *International Journal of Sports Physiology and Science*, (2013) No. 8, p. 639–47.

Chapter 9 Beating the Winter Greys and Blues

1 Adding weighted running vest has recently been advocated in published Ironman research on age-group athletes to help their running ability during a targeted training programme.
2 'What I termed hyper-gravity training' by Joe Beer, published in *Cycling Plus*, February 1997.
3 Many sections of *Time-Crunched Triathlete* were written with a light box at 60 centimetres away and angled at roughly 30 degrees. Increasing light up to 2,500–6,000 lux depends on how you angle the light metre. Bear in mind average levels, middle of the day, on a dark October day of 300–800 lux. Every little (bit of light) helps!

Chapter 10 Coping with Injury

1 For the record, Lee went on to win his age-group at the World Duathlon Championship in 2013 and again in 2014. And he won PowerMan Arizona 2015 outright, ahead of all the professional athletes. From the depths of that March he played the long game and months later was back to his very best.
2 Dave finished Ironman Wales to get his dozen Ironman finishes and entered Ironman Lanzarote 2015. He is also finding new areas to focus on, mainly thanks to InDurance blood profiling.
3 After Chris went on to become a dad (twice), he won the Powerman UK 2014 and the Cotswold 113. Nor is he planning to slow down any time soon. We are both continuing to learn how to best adapt his programme and be time-efficient.

GLOSSARY

adaptation the process of transforming exercise into a positive gain in a physical ability (e.g. increased endurance), achieved by the correct balance of training load and nutrition

aerobar also known as 'Tri Bar', these are extensions that go forwards from the handlebar to allow the rider to rest his or her forearms on padded cups while riding, resulting in improved aerodynamics and an upper body that is rested

age-group athletes non-professionals who race against their peers of a similar age, a very small percentage of whom go on to become professionals in their teens or early twenties

anaerobic threshold (AT) the heart rate point at which strenuous 'race pace' exercise can be sustained for around one hour; above this point, chemical by-products build up in the body to slow down the athlete, but may recover to surge again above threshold

ATP–CP system the adenosine triphosphate and phosphocreatine bonds, which can unleash high-power efforts (for example, when sprinting for ten seconds)

autonomic system the body's unconscious control system that regulates organs and muscles such as the heart, bladder and kidneys

base training training at skill practice; longer endurance sessions or back-to-back work (e.g. bike, run, bike, run...) with a heart rate from 60–80 per cent of HRmax

bonk a significant drop in blood sugar which the athlete senses as a drop in short-term motivation and energy levels; may be transient due to nutrition timing beforehand or indicating a long session has been poorly supported with carbohydrate feeding

bpm beats per minute (see **heart rate**)

bricks a run that occurs soon after a bike session; may be one single run (e.g. one hour bike + 20 minute run) or multiple back-to-back efforts (e.g. 6 × stationary gym bike + treadmill, 5 minutes of each)

carbohydrate-loading a 3–5 day period of increased carbohydrate content in the diet and reduced training volume to increase glycogen levels in the muscle

creatine also known as creatine monohydrate, a sports supplement that, when taken for sufficient time, will increase ability in short burst efforts and intervals, such as weight training

colostrum the first milk produced by a cow, forming the primary food for its calves

diuretic a substance that increases the urine losses from the body and therefore may be considered as a factor in de-hydration

ergogenics also known as ergogenic aids, these are equipment, nutritional manipulation or psychological practices which may improve sports performance, whether legally or illegally

ergolytics any nutrition, drugs or practices that impair performance, such as excessive alcohol, harmful drugs

Functional Threshold Power (FTP) often used interchangeably with **Threshold Power** and **anaerobic threshold (AT)** by users of bicycle power measuring systems; is around 85–90 per cent of **HRmax**

Glycogen carbohydrate and water in the diet combined and stored in muscle, liver and brain to be used as fuel by exercising muscle

heart rate (HR) the number of contractions (or beats) per minute; differences between people are common, but generally the heart rate is 25–75 bpm at rest and 160–225 bpm at maximum

high cadence work where a typical cycling training cadence of 85–95 rpm is replaced with intervals of faster leg motion (95–115 rpm), but not necessarily at a very high effort if a suitable easy gear is chosen

high-intensity effort (HIT) any effort that occurs above **anaerobic threshold**; typically around 87–92 per cent of **HRmax**

high-intensity interval training (HIIT) a type of **HIT** divided into intervals

HRmax the maximum heart rate, in beats per minute (**bpm**), achieved at the end of a progressive exercise test, often assisted by a coach or a sports scientist

hunger knock a drop in energy and mood when calorie intake over a long session drops past a critical point

interval training non-continuous training using a varied pace to 'work' then 'recover or refocus', e.g. skill-based technical intervals at moderate intensity with very low intensity between or HIIT as above

lactate buffering the process in muscle and blood uses lactate as a useful fuel source to aid muscle to continue to contract

lactate level the amount of lactate (also wrongly known as lactic acid) occurring in an athlete's muscle and bloodstream and which aids energy production in muscle,

not retards it; at rest, blood lactate this is ~1mmol, at anaerobic threshold this is 4 mmol, and at maximal effort this is 7–15 mmol.

low cadence work (see **over-geared riding**) where typical training cycling cadence of 85–95 rpm is replaced with intervals of pedalling a harder gear at a lower cadence (50–60 rpm)

maximum power output often refers to the highest one-minute value, in watts, sustained at the end of a progressive cycling power test, e.g. 389 watts

millimole (mmol) unit of measurement for minute levels of substances in blood, such as lactate and glucose

over-geared efforts (OGE), see **over-geared riding**

over-geared riding (also known as **over-geared efforts**) using a low cadence and a harder gear than that which the athlete would freely choose; typically, 50–60 revolutions per minute (rpm) for intervals of 1 to 8 minutes

recovery drink a mixture of carbohydrate and protein powder that mixes with water to maximize recovery in the first 2–4 hours after a hard session

recovery interval (RI) a period of time between one HIIT effort and the next; the recovery between weight-training exercises

reps repetitions (reps)

rpm revolutions per minute

sarcopenia the loss of muscle that occurs with ageing and lack of physical exercise

stationary trainer session, see **turbo session**

Strava ego the habit of training faster than optimal due to social media reporting of an athlete's training data; unfortunately, this is a good tool used to create a poor long-term outcome

submax (also known as **sub-maximal**) often used to describe steady state or controlled training or fitness

testing that stays below threshold (<85 per cent HRmax)

submaximal, see **submax**

tapering reducing the length, frequency and possibly intensity of a training session in the final 7–20 days before a race, depending on the length of the race and the maximum training load the athlete has achieved

tempo training often used to describe faster training efforts though these are not as hard as HIIT; close to race pace, this will often result in a HR in Zone 2 (81–6 per cent HRmax)

Threshold Power, see **Functional Threshold Power**

transient hypoglycaemia a short-term drop in blood sugar that may occur early in exercise in some athletes; assuming a doctor has given the athlete the all-clear prior to exercise, this is annoying but not harmful or indicative of anything serious

transition the actions of movement between the end of swimming when a triathlete stands up and the point at which they mount the bike to cycle; also the point when the athlete dismounts the cycle and begins running out of the transition area to begin the run section of the race

tri-bar riding the act of riding on tri bars or aerobars to get used to the handling, change of muscular pressure and saddle pressure that occurs when an athlete is used to riding a standard cycling position

turbo session (also known as **stationary trainer session**) an indoor cycling exercise either with a normal bicycle attached to a frame (e.g. Tacx Magnetic Trainer) or using a stationary device (e.g. Wattbike)

VO$_2$max the maximum amount of oxygen that an athlete's exercising muscles can process, per minute, expressed in litres or millilitres per kilogram of bodyweight

INDEX